INDIE AUTHOR CONFIDENTIAL 6

SECRETS NO ONE WILL TELL YOU ABOUT WRITING

M.L. RONN

ABOUT THIS SERIES

This isn't your typical writing self-help book. This series is a compilation of lessons learned from an indie author trying to walk the path to success. Follow author M.L. Ronn (Michael La Ronn) as he navigates what it means to master the craft of writing, marketing, and running a profitable publishing business. Learn from his successes and failures, and learn about things that most successful authors only talk about behind the scenes.

To read all the collected volumes of this series in an anthology, visit www.authorlevelup.com/confidential.

CONTENTS

BECOME A TECHNOLOGY AND DATA-DRIVEN WRITER

BECOME THE WRITER OF THE FUTURE

INTRODUCTION

In the last volume, I wrote about how a major life change kept me from writing for a brief time during Q2. I'm making up for it with this volume, as I'm back to normal. In fact, I'm better than normal because I'm doing another "Beast Mode Challenge" this year, with a goal of writing at least 10 books in 90 days.

In Q2 of this year, I wrote the *Indie Author Confidential* volume book late in the quarter. In Q3, I decided to write the volume early in the quarter so I could focus on Beast Mode. I technically wrote part of this book during Beast Mode, and I'll be publishing it in the middle of the challenge.

By writing most of this volume before the busiest days of the challenge, I'll stay on schedule. Last year, a lot of items fell off my radar during Beast Mode. This year, I don't want the *Indie Author Confidential* series to be one of those things.

I'll share the results of the Beast Mode Challenge in the next volume, but in the meantime, I've got a great volume for you that ventures into both familiar and new territory.

My Core Strategic Priorities

As a refresher, my mission is to create content that entertains and/or educates my audience, preferably both, and to remain nimble in an ever-changing industry. I do this by focusing on five strategic priorities:

- Become a world-class content creator
- Become a world-class marketer
- Become a technology-driven writer
- Become a data-driven writer
- Become the writer of the future

I believe these five priorities are most important for me to have a long-term, sustainable career.

What's in This Volume

As usual, you'll find sections for each of my strategic pillars, though Technology and Data and have been combined.

In the World-Class Content Creation section, I discuss my preparation for Beast Mode, why I don't write every day, and some thoughts on wrapping up teaching insurance classes, which helped me become a better public speaker.

In the World-Class Marketer section, I discuss experiments with permafree and pricing psychology. I also write about my most ridiculous pitch of all time.

In the Technology and Data section, I discuss thoughts on the new writing app Atticus, artificial intelligence and why authors aren't interested in hearing about it, and more nuanced thoughts about backing up my data.

In the Writer of the Future, I discuss more adventures in AI as well as a new segment where I look back at my writing career one year, five years, and ten years ago. I also discuss the potential ramifications of big tech legislation in the United States and it will almost certainly impact indie authors in the short and long term. And, in a series first, I discuss thoughts on death and what it means to be an author after the death of my grandfather.

2021 has been a decent year so far and I'm hoping that the progress I made this quarter will help me finish the year strong.

Enjoy this volume.

M.L. Ronn
July 15, 2021
Des Moines, Iowa

BECOME A WORLD-CLASS
CONTENT CREATOR

HOW I MASTERED REPURPOSING (AGAIN)

The previous volume of this series was the last to contain an "Ideas You Can Steal" section.

I had an idea to create a new book with just the "Ideas You Can Steal" from the first five volumes of this series. My goal was to use them to compile a fresh book that would have separate marketing potential and a life of its own.

Good ideas should be shared. I don't know if the ideas I posed in this series are good or not, but I figured I might as well send them into the world to find out. There was also the slight chance that this book could bring new readers onto my platform, but I didn't design the book with that goal in mind.

The book was titled *Authors, Steal This Book: 67 Business Ideas for the Writers of the Future.*

I made the book permafree to make it easier to spread the ideas. However, I had to accept the major downside of permafree: bad reviews. Readers who get books for free are far more likely to leave harsher reviews. But if there was any book where I welcomed bad reviews, it was this one.

I knew in advance that some people were going to read it and say, "This book didn't make me any money. I wanted actionable strategies to sell more books that work TODAY, not visions of the future." There are always going to be those people who completely miss the point of a book, even though you beat them over the head with it.

The reviews I care about are the ones that say, "This was an engaging book of ideas, but I agreed/didn't agree with the ideas because..."

We benefit when we engage in meaningful dialogue about what we want the author profession to be in several decades. Whether readers agree with me or not, if my book makes people start thinking about this and assert their own opinions about what they want the future to look like, then the book will have done its job.

When you write as many books as I do, your goals change. I've never written a book that advances a philosophy (for free) before, so this was a fun experiment.

Also, you never know who will read your books. It could create opportunities for me, or even better, one of the ideas might become reality! If that happens, we all win.

Will it work? It's too soon to tell, but I'm glad I published the book.

Authors, Steal This Book was stunningly simple to create. It required almost no effort to produce.

It took me an hour to write the introduction. I slipped it in with my manuscript for *Indie Author Confidential Vol. 5* when I sent it to my editor.

It took an hour to research a good image for the cover.

It took three days to get the cover designed.

It took 30 minutes to compile all the ideas from the previous volumes in this series into Vellum (my formatting software), and another 30 minutes to proof everything.

And boom—new book with minimal cost and effort. Fully edited and with a cover quality that my readers typically expect.

And it fits right in with the other books in my writing guide series.

That's how you can take content that you've already created, repurpose and repackage it, and use it to reach a new audience. If there's anything I've learned in this business, it's that you NEVER know who is going to come into contact with your books out in the wild. If you understand that, then you understand that it's in your best interest to put as much out there as possible. If, from time to time, you can repackage something with minimal effort, it's a smart win. (But remember, don't nickel and dime your audience, and don't be deceitful about it. A lot of marketers give repurposing a bad name.)

At the end of 2021, the *Indie Author Confidential* series will be a substantial property with seven volumes, two omnibuses (Volumes 1-3 and Volumes 4-7), and a spinoff book with the ideas. Pretty amazing what you can do if you get creative.

If you're interested, you can grab *Authors, Steal This Book* at www.authorlevelup.com/stealthisbook.

WHAT IT LOOKS LIKE WHEN YOU HAVE AN INTERESTING IDEA

In the previous volume, I wrote about "amalgamating" a series, which meant mashing two series together to create a new one. The new series would contain hybrids of the characters, worlds, and settings. I was fascinated by the idea.

As I reflected on it, I realized that this was a rare idea with a clear provenance.

Often, my ideas have multiple sources and it's weird how they come together. I don't often stop to think about HOW my ideas are formed, but this one is pretty fun.

- I was reminiscing on old-school comic books, and I remembered the *Amalgam* series by DC and Marvel. They fused their iconic characters into one. Batman + Wolverine = Dark Claw. Superman + Captain America = Super-Soldier. And so on.
- A few days before that, one of my series suddenly spiked on Amazon. It rose to #1 in its categories and it came out of nowhere. To this day, I still have no idea what precipitated the sales boost.

- In a recent livestream on my YouTube channel, someone asked me if my ideas are inspired by real-life or if I just make them up. I answered that I get inspiration from my personal life.
- Around this same time, I had some construction done at my house and the contractors tore up my grass pretty badly. They laid down sod, so I had to water it every day. The roots started "establishing," which means they were digging into my soil, which is a major step in the development of sod because you can mow it and reduce the watering.

PUTTING IT ALL TOGETHER: A NEW SERIES IDEA

Idea 1.A: What if I took two of my existing fiction series and mashed them together? Take both protagonists and fuse their personalities and timelines? What if I did the same with the supporting characters, villains, and settings?

Idea 1.B: What if I used this new "amalgamated" series as a marketing tool for my existing two series? In other words, if it becomes popular, it will automatically increase the sales of my existing series. If any of my existing series become popular in the future, readers will LOVE the amalgamation!

Idea 1.C: Because both worlds are already written, do I need to write into the dark or is the story more of a creative exercise? In other words... do I need to OUTLINE THIS SERIES to stay true to both worlds while also pushing them in a new and original direction?

In theory, readers already know what happens in at least one of the worlds, but not the new one. The new one will always "feel" familiar, but it won't quite be.

With Writing into the Dark, the key philosophy is that "If you don't know what will happen, then readers won't either." Fusing both worlds would achieve that goal.

I can use outlining as a STRATEGIC TOOL to deliver maximum fan service. It's also an example that every writing technique is merely a tool. If you've followed me for a while, you know that I have strong feelings about writing into the dark, and I haven't outlined in years. But maybe this is the right time to pull out the tool and use it unusually. All I care about is telling a great story and taking readers on a fun ride. I'm not above using any tool to help me do that.

Will I outline my novels moving forward? Heck no, but this could be an interesting experiment.

Idea 1.D: Maybe I just need to outline the series up to a certain point, and then the "roots" of the series (i.e. reader expectations) will be established, allowing me to write the rest of the series into the dark.

That's how this idea formed. I haven't written the series yet, but it's high on my priority list because I'm excited about it. If it fails, it will at least have been fun. If it succeeds, it could make an amazing amount of money and grow my readership exponentially.

You can steal this idea too.

A NOVEL WITH NO CHAPTERS

Many book ideas come to me when I listen to jazz. In the previous volume, I wrote about Casiopea, my favorite Japanese jazz fusion band. I was listening to their 2004 *Marble* album, which was the last studio album before the band went on a hiatus. The first track, "Universe," is a 25-minute-long magnum opus that takes you on a journey through the universe. There are no breaks, and the band plays the song in one take. There are complicated chord changes, complex rhythms, and very technical solos. The entire song is a tour de force in jazz fusion, and every time I listen to it, I'm amazed by the band's musicianship.

That got me thinking about an interesting idea for fiction. What if I wrote a novel with no chapters? What if it were a story told in one continuous take? What kind of character would this be about? What craft techniques would I have to use to keep readers engaged?

Readers expect chapters. Almost every book is written using them. I think it would be fun to write a book that didn't.

I know I'm not the first to try this, but it would be a fun challenge.

When I wrote poetry, I used to challenge myself to write in different poetic forms. I would pick a form and then figure out what the poem would be about. Sometimes it worked, sometimes it didn't, but I find that I am a content-first person. Typically, I decide what type of story I'm going to write, and then the form follows. It's fun to do it the other way around sometimes.

I'm still mulling this idea over, and it may be a long time before I implement it. You're welcome to steal it.

BOOK COMMENTARY

In 2014, I created a reader bonus that I forgot about until now. I called it "book commentary."

This makes me feel old, but I used to collect DVDs. One of my favorite bonus features was director commentary. It was an audio track that, when chosen, would play over the movie or television show, and the director would talk about the inspiration to the story and how scenes were filmed. The commentary was always fascinating to me. I don't understand why it stopped in the streaming era. Netflix and Hulu's failure to implement it was a blow to the creative arts.

I still owned DVDs in 2014, so commentary was fresh on my mind. For my novels *Theo and the Festival of Shadows* and *Food City* (formerly *Eaten Season 1*), I recorded author commentary and linked to it from special sections of the book. *Theo and the Festival of Shadows* is an interactive novel, and the commentary was a bonus feature that the reader unlocked if they beat an interactive board game.

I listened to the commentary again after all these years, and it was fun to relive it. I sounded stiff behind the microphone. I didn't have good gear, and my execution could have been better. Almost no one listened to the commentary.

What if I brought this back for my novels again, and linked to a five-minute video where I talked about the inspiration behind the novel? What if I did this with my writing books? It's an interesting thought now that I have a bigger readership.

HOW I BUILT A SUCCESSFUL WRITING BUSINESS (WITHOUT WRITING EVERY SINGLE DAY)

On my nightly blog, I report my daily word counts, even if I don't write any words for that day.

Last quarter, there were several days where I wasn't able to write. I posted my zero numbers, and I didn't make any excuses for them. Rather, I felt it gave my audience a realistic view of what the part-time writing life was like.

I don't remember the exact number of days, but in May, I probably only wrote on 10 days. The rest were zero-word count days.

Why? I started a new job, I finished law school, and I had some other personal issues to attend to. Those things prevented me from writing.

That's okay. I want people to know that you can have a prolific writing career even if you don't write every day. Many people (including aspiring writers) think they are failures if they don't write every day. They have quotas, and if they don't hit those quotas, their day is ruined.

Don't get me wrong—I'm not against quotas. Prolific writer James Scott Bell advocates for them, and I agree with his reasoning that prolific writers who write day in and day out will have long careers.

I just don't believe in hard quotas. I don't get angry if I want to write a chapter and fail to do so. That's the key.

In my book *Be a Writing Machine*, I talk about the law of averages. Let's say that I only wrote on 10 days every month of the year, and let's say that I wrote 1,000 words each day. That's 10,000 words per month and 120,000 words per year. If you write 50,000-word novels, that's 2.4 novels per year, which is a respectable number. In a decade, that will net you 24 novels, which is more than many writers write in their entire careers.

Keep in mind that those numbers are based on writing only 10 days per month. I happen to think that those numbers are fantastic.

If we bump up our daily word count streak to 20 days per month, that gets us 20,000 words per month and 240,000 words per year, which equates to 4.8 novels per year and 48 novels in a decade. Again, those are fantastic numbers, and we are merely assuming a small word count per day and a 66 percent daily writing rate.

Multiply those numbers by a 30-year-long writing career, and by the time you die, you will have published 144 novels. That easily puts you in the upper echelon of the most prolific writers who have ever lived.

Increase your daily word count numbers and you will become exponentially more prolific—and you're only writing 20 days per month.

Increase the number of days per month you write, and you'll also become more prolific—and you're only writing 1,000 words per day.

That's how the law of averages works. As long as you continue to sit down in the chair, it will work in your favor. Most people don't see it that way, though.

The numbers I described are inspiring and cumulative, yet writers still beat themselves up because life happened and they couldn't write on a Saturday afternoon.

I've written over 60 books while raising a family, working a demanding job in the insurance industry, and attending law school classes in the evenings. If I can write this many books (as a part-time writer) and be considered prolific, then you can too. You can even do better than me if you follow the advice above.

But remember your priorities.

First things first: your family comes before anything else. If you have small children (or big children for that matter) and they need something, take care of them. Same with your spouse, aging parents, relatives, and so on. Your children will only be in the house for so many years and you only have your parents and grandparents for so long.

Second, your day job also takes priority. Why? Because if you're a new writer who is paying out of pocket for producing your books, if you don't have a day job, you can't afford to publish at the quality readers expect. Once you have more books, this changes. If you hate your day job, find another day job.

I'm now an executive at a global insurance company, yet here I am still writing books. There are a lot of days when work makes bigger demands of me than the regular 9 to 5. That's okay. I have a very high tolerance level when it comes to working. I thrive under pressure. My path is not for the faint of heart.

If that's not you and you can leave your work at work, then do that.

Third, you don't have to write every day to have a career as a writer. I've written almost 60 books at this point, and I didn't get here by writing every day.

Sometimes, I had family obligations or work obligations or law school, or something else. I didn't write every day. Many weeks, I did, but there were some weeks and months where I didn't write at all. Or, I'd eke out 100-word days. Yet, I still managed to write 60 books and make pretty good money with my writing. The key is that I always kept at it, even if I failed some days.

I never get upset or worried if I don't write on a certain day. And trust me, with Beast Mode coming up, I'm going to miss on some days. Any deadlines in this business are self-made. No one will prosecute me if I miss a quota.

Don't worry about zero-word count days. Take that energy and focus it on whatever made you miss because that's where your attention should be *anyway*...then pick yourself back up and try again.

(And no, I don't care what anyone says about NaNoWriMo —no one will die if you don't write a 50,000-word novel in November. Use challenges like NaNoWriMo to motivate and inspire you, but they aren't worth it if you stress yourself out. In all the public challenges I have done, I've had tons of fun whether I succeeded or failed. Big difference.)

I'm not saying that you should never write, or that you should be lazy and find excuses not to write. You all know that I believe the exact opposite, and I hopefully have led by example in this area.

This is why I'm such an advocate for writing on your phone or dictating. Sometimes that can mean the difference between a zero-day and a productive day. Add enough of those days together and you have a career.

Be intentional about your writing. Write as much as you can when you can, and remember the law of averages. Even if you miss a few days or weeks, you'll more than likely have word count days that even out your yearly word count.

If you never thought about your yearly word count, then you should. A career equals many years, hopefully decades if you're young enough. Some years, you'll be down. Some years, you'll be up. In 2017, I wrote 12 books, and 9 of those were novels, which is insane. In 2020, I did 10 books, mostly nonfiction, but it was still an equally productive year. In 2018, I only wrote 5 books. 2021 will probably be somewhere between 10 to 12. Take advantage of the good years and good times and wait out the bad ones. Despite what you think, no one's watching, and no one cares except you. I find that freeing.

And take care of yourself. There's no point writing 10 books a year if you burn yourself out. The reason I don't burn out is that I keep my writing fun.

Sure, it's true that if you write every single day without fail, you will write more books and (maybe) even make more money. But I'd rather write as much as I can (with zero days from time to time) if it means I'm balanced in all areas of my life instead of writing every day and burning out. Life happens. Even with the best plans and organization, you're going to get knocked down. Just roll with it.

I've been a published author for almost a decade, and I've met a lot of indie authors. I don't know any who can sustain a breakneck pace for very long without burning out. Not a single one.

There are people in the community who believe in writing every day without fail, and if that works for them, fine, but that doesn't mean YOU have to do it. Sure, aspire to it, but don't be angry if you fail at it.

"But, Michael! If I take too long between publishing books, readers will forget about me!!!!!!"

Do you think anyone forgot about George R. R. Martin between *A Game of Thrones* books? If he can get away with taking two decades to write that series, then you can get away with anything. Build your email list and your community, keep in touch with your fans, and stay diligent.

"But, Michael! If I don't publish often, the algorithms will send my first books to hell!!!"

So be it. Again, as someone who has been doing this for almost a decade with a lot of books and sales to show for it, I can tell you that a book isn't worth sacrificing for the other areas in your life.

Your writing will always be there. That's part of its charm. It's something you can always escape to and turn to in hard times. No matter what happens to you, you will always be a writer if you write.

Your writing will always be there. That's not necessarily true about your spouse, children, or your health.

We aren't immune to the influence of hustle culture in the indie community. Don't let someone talk you into doing anything that doesn't work for you. Anyone can talk a good hustle game, but at the end of the day, you're the one that has to live your career.

THE ULTIMATE GUIDE TO WRITER'S BLOCK

I published the following chapter in my *Writing Tips* series, and I thought it would be great to include it here since a lot of people are always thinking about writer's block and how to beat it. Enjoy.

———

Ah, the dreaded writer's block. Every writer must learn to deal with it in some form. While it would be awesome if the words flowed from our brains to our fingers in one smooth motion, it often doesn't happen that way. It can feel like a downright battle to beat writer's block, especially in difficult parts of a book like the murky middle.

You can never banish writer's block, but you can minimize its impacts. This chapter is dedicated to helping you beat writer's block every time it comes around.

The Root Causes of Writer's Block

. . .

Writer's block is a response, not an emotion. I believe it's your spirit (or the universe, or God, or whatever you believe in spiritually) telling you that something is wrong. Not with you, but with your story.

Dean Wesley Smith, a prolific writer, often says that your brain (or your creative voice) knows everything about writing a story; when you read, you learn subconsciously. When you write, much of that subconscious learning flows out automatically. The key is to be aware of what you're learning so you can recognize what your creative voice is doing. I agree with that assessment.

Your creative voice knows everything about writing a story; it also knows when something is wrong. When it can't continue, it throws up a roadblock, stopping you from continuing. At that point, it's *your* job to figure out what's wrong and to give your creative voice what it needs to continue.

To understand what your creative voice needs, it's helpful to understand the three root causes of writer's block.

The first root cause is fear. Everyone deals with fear to some extent. You might be afraid that you can't tell a good story, or that you'll never be able to finish your book, or that readers won't want to buy it, or that you'll receive bad reviews, and so on. Fear is especially difficult to deal with because it changes based on the context. A new writer deals with fear in the same quantity as a mega-bestseller, but the *type* of fear is different. That's what people misunderstand about it. Many think, "If I could just finish my book or become a full-time writer, my problems will go away forever." That never happens.

When you understand that fear will always be with you, you'll have a healthier and more realistic toolbox to beat it. If you treat fear as an ever-morphing foe, you'll be able to recognize it every time it appears.

Fear creates writer's block, and in my opinion, it is the

predominant root cause. The best way to address fear is to fight it.

The second root cause is a lack of inspiration. Sometimes your creative voice needs inspiration to keep going. If you've ever driven a car and ran low on gas, you can probably relate to this: you're driving a car, and suddenly, the low gas light comes on. You start panicking about whether you can reach the nearest gas station before your car shuts off. If you're on a road trip, you become especially nervous. Every mile feels like ten until you see the tall, bright sign of a gas station on the side of the road. You pull up to the pump, fill up the car, and drive off, relieved.

Suffering from a lack of inspiration is the same way. Writer's block is like the gas light that switches on suddenly. It changes the tenor of your drive until you fix it. You're running out of figurative gas, and you need it fast.

The best way to combat this problem is to keep reading regularly. This way, you're filling up your writer's tank so that you always have a rich pool of ideas to draw from.

The third root cause is personal circumstances. Sometimes life happens, and it can take you away from writing for a time. Stress, sickness, death, financial issues, loss of a job, and other personal circumstances can halt your writing efforts. Even if you sit down to write, you'll find that your mind is elsewhere. The best way to deal with this cause is to address life head on. Once you take care of your problems, you'll find that the writer's block will go away.

Those are the three root causes of writer's block, but we won't stop there. Now we need to design some strategies to help you win the war.

Developing Strategies Against Fear

. . .

First, don't believe anything fear says.

I have a theory: when you write, you become a child. You transport yourself back to your childhood, where everything was possible and there were no bad ideas. Being able to "play" is an essential part of being a creative, and writers know how to access their inner child for maximum benefit.

When readers read, they become children too. Action, adventure, love, and thrill takes them back to their childhoods.

In my mind, writing and reading is just a conversation between children.

However, when you become a child, you invite all the baggage from your childhood to the surface too. So much trauma happens in childhood, and it's easy to push it aside and not address it. For example, if you had difficult relationships with your parents as a child, that will manifest itself in your personality when you become an adult. If you were bullied on the playground, that will have an effect too. We all have our traumas, and sometimes trauma doesn't look like you think it will look. Sometimes it's merely someone saying something to you, and you don't realize the damage until years later.

When you become a child and return to the land of writing, where everything is fun and possible, trauma is never far away. It follows you like a whispering shadow. Sometimes it overtakes you, and that makes you freeze.

The best way to deal with trauma is to face it. If you don't know what your traumas are, you have to find them. But more often than not, you know what they are. Whatever your inner critic says to you when you write is a trauma. Things like "You'll never finish because you don't know how to tell a story," or, "No one will buy my work because..." or "I'm incapable of writing a love story because..."

Whatever excuses your critical voice throws at you, they're probably rooted in your childhood. This is my theory—if I'm right, then the solution is just a matter of human psychology. Once you face the trauma, it becomes easier to manage. It'll still follow you, but you'll ensure that the shadow never engulfs your inner child. Healing your traumas will make your inner child feel safer.

If you struggle to deal with your traumas, I recommend that you seek therapy. Don't listen to people who say that therapy is bad. Therapy is amazing—you get to talk to a stranger who is trained to listen and reflect your thoughts and feelings to you so you can understand yourself as you are, not who you *think* you are.

Understanding yourself and engaging in self-healing is one of the healthiest and most effective ways to fight fear. Fear thrives on a lack of awareness of oneself. When you don't understand *why* something throws you into an emotional rollercoaster, fear will take advantage of that.

To use another analogy, let's use a common fact of pest control. Pretend you have an opossum living under your porch, or a family of mice in your attic. Generally, pests don't like the presence of humans. They try to find places where they can live without interruption. If a pest lives in an abandoned house, and suddenly people move in and start living there, the pest is going to leave and find somewhere else to live. They preferred darkness where there is now light, and quiet where there is now constant noise. Fear is the same way.

Illuminate the darkest spaces of your heart, and fear will have fewer places to dwell.

Developing Strategies Against Lack of Inspiration

. . .

As I mentioned before, reading and consuming content regularly is the best inoculation against lack of inspiration. Your creative voice loves it when you're constantly exposing yourself to new stories and ideas.

To use another cheesy analogy, it's like putting hair food in your hair. It makes your hair richer and look better.

I find that capturing ideas is also another effective way to combat a lack of inspiration. For example, I use Evernote to write down ideas that come to me during the day. I write the idea down, file it away, and whenever I suffer from a lack of inspiration, I can refer to my Evernote account for a quick boost. I've accumulated thousands of ideas over the years, so much that I rarely deal with a lack of inspiration anymore.

I take pictures of interesting sights, write down unique things that people say (especially in dialect), scribble ideas that come to me at three AM, and so much more. Over the years, those notes have added up in a big way.

Let's express treatment to lack of inspiration with an equation: Regular consumption of content + capture + catalogue of ideas over time = reduced lack of inspiration. You can almost never go wrong if you follow this equation.

Other smart strategies to combat this root cause are meeting new people and visiting new places regularly. There's nothing like the rush of new people and new places to inspire your writing.

More Strategies to Beat Writer's Block

Now that we've covered tactics to help you beat each root cause, let's talk about advanced strategies. These tips are most effective once you've published a few books, and they can help you fight writer's block and fear as they morph.

The first strategy is to understand where you are in the process. Where does writer's block hit you the most? I find that it typically likes to visit at certain parts of a novel more than others, and that might be true for you too. For example, I tend to encounter writer's block without fail around the 20 to 30 percent mark of my novel. This is right around the point where the "honeymoon phase" and infatuation with a new project wears off. Writer's block strikes again around the 50 to 60 percent mark, usually in the darkest part of the "murky middle." Because I know this, I can plan for it. Usually, at the end of each writing day, I'll tally up my total word count for the novel and try to *predict* when the writer's block will probably come. For example, if I write 1,000 words a day and my novels are usually 50,000 words, I can expect to run into writer's block sometime around 10,000 to 12,000 words. So, if it's Monday and I'm at 7,000 words, I can almost certainly expect to run into a rough patch sometime before the weekend.

Planning is the key. If you treat writer's block like a rainstorm, you'll treat it differently. If you planned a party in your backyard, you'd move it indoors for a rainstorm, right? If you expect writer's block to arrive within a few days, you might reschedule some of your life so that you can be ready for it.

The second strategy is to visualize the future and what will be once you've conquered writer's block. If you can visualize a problem, you can solve it. I like to imagine the problem as a physical ball of tangled yarn, and I imagine myself untangling the yarn. That helps.

The third strategy is to lean into writer's block when appropriate. It's like driving a car and skidding out of control. The best thing to do is to lean into the skid; it's counterintuitive but works every time. Sometimes you should lean into writer's block. Set the writing aside and "drift" for a few days, always on the lookout for inspiration. Just make sure you return to your manuscript!

The fourth strategy is to listen to the writer's block. Is your creative voice trying to tell you something? Is there something else you should be doing instead, such as dealing with a personal crisis? This seems odd, but I find that writer's block often happens a day or so *before* life strikes. It's like it knows when things will go awry. I've learned to listen and be a student of my creative voice, always attenuating myself to its needs.

Remember, writer's block is an emotional response.

The fifth strategy is to approach writer's block like a United States Navy SEAL. Navy SEALs are some of the toughest soldiers in the world, and they endure training that would be unbearable to most people. During boot camp, the most successful seals are those who can adopt "microfocus." Instead of focusing on finishing boot camp, they focus instead on moving their arm while they're crawling through the mud in a thunderstorm. You too can develop microfocus. Instead of focusing on the book, focus on writing the next sentence.

The sixth strategy to develop amnesia about your writer's block. If you're dealing with writer's block, just forget it. Pretend it doesn't exist. A year from now, when your book has been published for a while, you won't even remember the sections that gave you the most trouble.

Also, your editor can't tell when you have writer's block. Once they're done with the book, everything will be so smooth that no one will even know where you struggled. Adopt that perspective while you're writing.

The seventh strategy is to think of writer's block as an experience that will make you a better writer. Every time you beat it, you're better for it. Adopt a curiosity mindset whenever writer's block appears and you'll be shocked at how your perspective changes. Be intentional about fighting it, keep sitting down and writing, try to keep momentum, and there will come a point where you will break through and you'll return to smoother writing sessions. You just have to have the courage to keep going.

You can win the war against writer's block. Fortunately, I have a lot of books that will help you.

How to Write Your First Novel is about helping you finish your first book.

Be a Writing Machine is about writing faster and smarter, beating writer's block, and being prolific. I delve into many of the strategies I discuss in this chapter.

Mental Models for Writers is about small mindset shifts that can make a big difference in your career.

The Indie Author Bestiary is a manual for conquering the "beasts" of the writing life, such as fear and self-doubt.

You can find all of my books for writers at www.author levelup.com/books.

TIME TO DO A CLEANUP

Last quarter, I published two books: *Indie Author Confidential Volume 5* and *Authors, Steal This Book*. As I was publishing them, I realized that the major retailer dashboards have changed slightly. Amazon introduced some new functionality on its pricing screen, and Google Play made some minor changes too.

I realized that it's time for another "patrol." I needed to review my books' sales pages to check:

- Metadata
- Prices for all formats
- Book descriptions (typos and formatting breaks only)
- Availability

I don't like doing this, but it's necessary. Things happen over the years. However, when you have over 60 books, these types of tasks become more challenging. I had to develop a plan.

- I can't do all of this by myself. I need help, which means I have to hire someone.

- I need to develop a checklist that covers the items that need to be reviewed.
- I need that checklist to stay mostly the same from year to year.
- I need to develop a "report" that the assistant can give me. I need to retain that report for future years so I can remember what was done for each book.

This is important so that I ensure:

- my books are available widely
- each format of my books is available widely
- the correct version of the book is available for sale
- my books are priced correctly across currencies
- no typos exist in the book description

This is going to be a lot of work, but I will try to accomplish it before the end of the year.

MAKING MINOR MODIFICATIONS TO THE PACKAGING OF THE INDIE AUTHOR CONFIDENTIAL SERIES

While we're on the topic of cleaning up my work, I noticed two minor issues with the *Indie Author Confidential* series that needed immediate rectification.

The first issue was that, when placing all the covers of this series side-by-side, I noticed a color mistake.

Volume 1 of this series had my author name in black text. Volumes 2 and onward had my name in white text. The white text looked much better and more appealing. When you looked at all the titles together, Volume 1 stood out in a bad way.

Most readers probably never noticed. I'm surprised it took me this long to see it. Normally, I catch these errors before the designer is done with the design. I should have caught this with Volume 2, but sometimes things happen. (Do you see why I believe in intellectual property management now?)

Having one author name in the series in a different color is a very minor issue that other authors would have ignored and fixed later, but for me, it was a matter of professionalism.

The second issue was that I forgot that Volume 1 had a call to action page called "Read Next: Vol. X." That page had the picture of the next volume in the series, two sentences of copy, and a link. I forgot to do this with Volume 2 onward. This is even less of a minor issue that I'm certain that almost no one observed. However, adding CTAs to the series is a smart sales tool. I was smart enough to do this for Volume 1, but somehow I forgot with the rest of the volumes.

Here are the steps I took to rectify both issues.

- I worked with my designer to update the color of the author name on Volume 1. I had him update the ebook cover, paperback cover, and source file so that everything was consistent. It cost me $10.
- For Volume 1, I updated the cover within the Vellum file and regenerated new editions of the book. I also updated the version on the copyright page to 2.0 and logged a note in my versioning system.
- For the omnibus containing Volumes 1 through 3, I included the covers as full-page spreads so the reader knows when they've arrived at a new volume. I changed Volume 1's cover here too. I regenerated new versions of the book and updated my version log.
- I updated the image of the cover on my website: on my books page, on the series page, and the individual book page.
- I updated the CTA for Volumes 2 through 5 so that they have links to the next book in the series when the reader finishes reading. I regenerated fresh versions of the books and updated my version log.
- I uploaded the new versions to all retailers. I went slowly and was extremely careful!
- One week later, I spot-checked the retailers to make sure the right versions were uploaded. I didn't check

them all because I'll be doing this as part of my next "patrol."

The entire update process took me approximately two hours. The result is that the series looks even more professional and it's poised to sell more copies.

This is the behind-the-scenes, unglamorous part of managing your books after publication.

LONG-FORM AUDIO CONTENT

I believe long-form audio content can do well. When I started podcasting in 2014, everyone said, "Keep your shows less than an hour. People are busy." It was rare to see any podcast in any industry go longer than an hour. Occasionally, a show might stretch to 90 minutes if the topic was popular.

Now more podcast episodes are two or three hours long. Podcasters are making longer content on average and people are tolerating it. I believe it's because people are more comfortable with the medium and willing to listen to personalities they love.

I also believe that there is no such thing as cycles in podcasting. Long-form content isn't going anywhere. It will coexist with short and medium forms. All forms have value.

People like short-form content when they need information. This is why my show, "Writing Tip of the Day" was popular. I delivered a writing tip in five minutes or less. It was my most popular podcast.

People like medium-form content because it fits neatly within the time it takes to complete many tasks. If you think about it, in the United States, the average commute is around 30 minutes one-way, so listeners can easily consume a 45- to 60-

minute show during that period. It takes, on average, the same amount of time to prepare a meal and clean up the kitchen. It also takes that amount to cut your lawn. And so on. Medium-form content is amazing for when you are multitasking. My show, "The Writer's Journey," was a medium-form show. It was also very popular.

Long-form content is good for multitasking as well, but I believe that people are mostly watching or actively listening to the content. It has their full attention. It is entertaining *and* informational. Livestreams are a good example of long-form content. My Writing Power Hours on my YouTube channel are an example—they run approximately 90 minutes in length, sometimes up to two hours.

We only have a few influencers in the self-publishing space who have ventured into long-form territory. I believe that the right person could find success if they're intentional about it.

THE DEATH OF THE OPEN RATE

Apple released a new iOS update that effectively kills the email open rate as we know it. I discuss this in detail in the next section.

However, because of this massive change, I needed to figure out if I had any sections in my writing books that talked about open rates so I could update them.

The following books needed updating:

- *150 Self-Publishing Questions Answered*
- *250 Writing Tips, Vol. 1*
- *Indie Poet Rock Star*
- *Mental Models for Writers*
- *The Indie Author Atlas*
- *The Indie Writer's Encyclopedia*

I updated the books accordingly to make them current. It took a few hours, but it's one less thing I have to worry about in the future.

That's what happens when you stick around in the writing

world for a few years. Things change, and you have to change
with them.

LESSONS FROM TEACHING
INSURANCE CLASSES

I taught my last insurance class, which closes a five-year-long journey that made a big impact on my personal development.

In this chapter, I wanted to recap the lessons I learned.

In 2016, I was a commercial underwriter. My job was to review businesses to verify if they were eligible for my company's commercial insurance products: general liability, commercial property, business auto, crime, cyber liability, and more. My manager at the time suggested that I go to a CIC class, which stands for Certified Insurance Counselor. It is a designation that insurance agents obtain to help them become more knowledgeable in insurance policies.

Before the pandemic, CIC classes were usually held in hotel conference rooms. For three days, you'd learn about the ins and outs of insurance policies, with a test at the end.

These days, the classes are mostly held online.

I didn't mind a change of scenery and it sounded like it could help me do my job better. Plus, my manager paid for it.

I attended the class and was blown away by the presenters. They made the most boring topics in the insurance world exciting. The speakers would present their material with wonderful stories rooted in their experience, and they held the audience spellbound. And best of all, their examples were clear and easy to understand.

I also met local insurance agents and other insurance industry professionals, which was a great networking opportunity.

(And, the hotel had *amazing* pretzels and cheese for the afternoon snack. I dream about those pretzels from time to time.)

I went to five classes and, in less than a year, I obtained my CIC designation. I asked one of the event organizers about becoming a faculty member, and they told me to apply on the website. The organizers were kind enough to give me a recommendation, so I landed an interview.

My interview was a phone call with the academic coordinator of the nonprofit organization that put on the events. I had no idea what to expect. The coordinator called me, and the interview started immediately. No small talk.

The interview questions they asked are forever burned into my brain.

"Please explain how limited worldwide coverage works on the general liability policy."

"Exclusion j4. What does it exclude?"

"Let's say, for the sake of argument, that one of my employees is driving their personal car on an errand for my business, and they get into a car accident. Would there be coverage under an unendorsed ISO business auto policy?"

Thank God I have an encyclopedic memory. I didn't have the insurance policies in front of me, but I aced the questions.

It went on like this for at least thirty minutes. They told me that I passed, but that I would have to undergo training, which took approximately one year. Then the coordinator explained the rules, which were quite strict.

My first assignment was a 200-slide PowerPoint in which I had to prepare clear examples for each slide. The slide went through the entire commercial general liability policy, line by line. I had a month to complete this assignment...in addition to working my job and writing books.

I came up with examples that explained the general liability policy as simply as I could. All of my examples were rejected. Over the course of several conference calls, the coordinator helped me craft examples that were better than anything I could have done myself. My PowerPoint slide deck went through at least three iterations until my examples were so clear and simple, they were almost childlike.

The next step was to practice my presentation. I prepared my remarks and practiced delivering them in front of the coordinator and a mentor. It seemed like every 10 seconds, they would stop me and try to stump me with a nuanced question.

"Michael, what about the exception to the exclusion you just mentioned?"

"Michael, X company offers Y product. That contradicts what you just said."

They would even ask me trick questions to knock me off-balance.

Honestly, the practice sessions were more like interrogation sessions. I met with them for two hours at a time, and after every session, I wanted to go home and take a nap. Somehow, however, I did well enough to move to the next phase, which was to teach a course under the tutelage of the mentor.

My first course went pretty well. I taught it in person, and I passed the evaluation with top marks. I was officially approved as a faculty instructor.

It was a crazy ride, and there were times I didn't think I would make it, but I persevered and joined the ranks of some of the most accomplished insurance industry speakers in the country.

The lessons I learned:

- Make your examples so clear that even a child can understand them. This is harder than it sounds.
- Prepare more examples than you need. Know when to pull them out.
- Anticipate people's questions ahead of time. You won't always be right, but when you are, you'll deepen your credibility with the group.
- When you give the same presentation over and over, you learn the material so well that your brain goes on autopilot. At the same time, this makes it much easier to read students' faces. When people look confused, that's when you slow down and ask if people understood what you just said.
- When people ask questions, always repeat the question. Always.
- Never tell students they're wrong. Soften your response by going through the material with them again. Otherwise, they will be defensive and they won't learn.
- Be as gender-neutral as you can. Even an innocent phrase like "guys" will upset some people.
- When presenting long-form content, take breaks every 50 minutes. Ten-minute breaks work best, and it's even better if you take breaks at the same time every hour. This way, people can plan around your breaks.
- To take care of yourself when speaking, eat breakfast but make sure you don't eat anything too

cold or too hot, as it will strain your vocal cords. Oatmeal is a perfect breakfast before you speak.

- Drink one water bottle every two hours. At each break, suck on a lozenge to protect your throat.
- If teaching from home, set up an essential oil diffuser and use a blend of eucalyptus and lemon to moisten and soften the air; this will make a huge difference in how long your vocal cords last. (Do not set up an essential oil diffuser if you are teaching in person.)
- Print your slides and always have paper copies. Sometimes Internet connections will derail you.
- Keep the webinar phone number handy in case you need to call in by telephone.
- At some point during an eight-hour course, your vocal cords are going to hurt. There's no way around it. The longer you can delay the exhaustion, the better. When I first started teaching, my voice would start hurting in the morning. Once I took better care of myself, my vocal cords wouldn't get tired until the course was almost over.
- For business-focus topics, it helps tremendously if you begin a talk with current events. Nothing gets people to pay attention more at 8 AM than something they probably heard about on the radio while driving into your class.
- The words you speak matter, but so does the tone.
- Try to be as engaging and personable as possible. It makes for a better class.

I learned many more lessons, but those are the ones that jumped out at me the most because I applied them immediately to my YouTube channel when I did live streams, and the techniques worked just as well on live streams as they do in the classroom. That's why I believe so much in liquid knowledge.

I may teach more classes someday. I enjoyed the people I worked with and I also enjoyed the students. I had an average faculty rating of 9.5 out of 10, and many students noted in their evaluations that my courses were some of the best they had ever attended. That makes me proud.

As I move to the next chapter of my writing career, I will carry these lessons with me.

WARMING UP FOR BEAST MODE

In the weeks leading up to my Beast Mode Challenge, I decided to practice and warm up to higher word counts.

There were also some events planned during Beast Mode that I needed to prepare for:

- A family vacation, so I had to prepare for writing on the go.
- Four speaking engagements during the 90-day Beast Mode period.
- A new school routine for my daughter in August, which would drastically change my household daily routine.

Since it had been a year since the last challenge, I figured I would start warming up early.

How did the first day go?

I normally start writing at 5:30 AM. I didn't start writing until 5 PM. I got a late start.

After I logged off work, I turned on my microphone and started dictating. I did 1,000 words in around 20 minutes, all clean. I ran the text through my editing engine and got it super crisp and editor-ready.

Then, it was time to water my sod, so I put in my Bluetooth headphones and opened Dragon Anywhere on my phone. I dictated another chapter while watering my lawn. That took about 10 minutes and it netted me 700 words. But boy, they were sloppy. Dictation gets you considerably worse results when you can't see the screen. I spent 15 minutes cleaning up those 700 words, which expanded it to about 900. I didn't like that, but I'll take the 700 words, even if they were bad.

After watering my sod and eating dinner, I did another dictation session and got another 1,500 words in about 30 minutes.

I did a final session by hand (typing) and got a remaining 800 words in about 20 minutes.

(And then I wrote an 800-word blog post. But I don't count those in my daily word counts. However, I did repurpose that blog post into this chapter, so I suppose I can count that blog post for a change.)

That's 4,000 words in one day. Not bad for a day with a late start.

That's how I warm up for Beast Mode: create a seamless transition between what I'm doing so that I can pick up my manuscript anywhere.

If I'm getting in an Uber? I whip out my phone and write.

If I gotta water my lawn? I dictate while I do it.

I dictate like my life depends on it when I'm sitting at my desk.

When I'm typing, I try to go as fast as I can without creating errors. I go faster than usual because I have a quiet urgency.

I did 4,000 words in an evening. Just think of what I can do with a morning that starts at 5:30 AM, and a lunch break. With perfect conditions, I could have easily hit 6,000 to 7,000 words without trying. In 2020, I hit 10,000 on at least one day during Beast Mode.

Of course, the words never come that easy except on a handful of days, and my word count days are considerably less when I'm writing fiction. But you can see how they add up. All you have to do is be intentional and just keep showing up. Amazing things happen when you do that.

BECOME A WORLD-CLASS MARKETER

IOS 15 AND EMAIL MARKETING

Apple announced iOS 15, which introduces new email privacy settings for iPhone and Apple Mail users. Users can opt in to hide their email and IP addresses, and they can also choose to block tracking pixels. This means that marketers will no longer be able to track reported open rates for Apple Mail users. It's being called a watershed moment in email marketing, and many marketers are freaking out.

When users open a newsletter, their email client downloads a pixel image. The pixel tells the person who sent the newsletter about whether the email was opened, in what email client, what device type, and where. Email pixels have been subject to privacy concerns for many years.

I don't think this will end email marketing. Open rates have always had issues. Users have been able to block images from emails for years, regardless of the email client. Some people prefer to read email in plain text to save Internet bandwidth. I've always known that if I achieve an open rate of 50 percent, the real number is higher than that because of pixel blocking. So, open rates have never been truly reliable anyway. This iOS update just exacerbates the problem.

I read somewhere that around 93 percent of email opens came from phones in 2020. If that's true, then customer preferences have changed significantly. People aren't tied to their desktop computers like they used to be.

That said, it's important to remember that this change is only for iOS users, who, while numerous, do not constitute the entire email universe. To my knowledge, Apple is the first to do this. They may not be the last, but for now, they're the only ones.

Also, my understanding is that click rates will still be tracked, and you don't need a pixel for that. Click rates are the ultimate metric that track engagement, and we still have it.

Many marketers are advising to do baseline tracking for subject lines, headers, calls to action, and so on. This way, they can track what's working and what's not after the iOS update sweeps across the world.

Here are my takeaways:

- Subscriber habits aren't changing per se; it's just that we won't be able to track them. It means that we'll be operating somewhat blindly with subject lines, for example. Candidly, I always thought A/B testing subject lines was always a pain in the ass anyway. While I don't like that I'm losing a data point, it does lessen the burden somewhat.
- Other email providers may follow Apple. If Google joins this trend, the open rate will be effectively dead.
- List hygiene will now be more difficult.
- This won't be the last assault on email marketing, but for now, there's no reason to change your behavior. Strong subject lines, well-written copy, and clear calls to action will still be effective.

I hoped that this would have a minimal impact on my email marketing, but approximately 21 percent of the people who open my emails do so with Apple Mail. That means that I need to stop looking at open rates, period. If I treat them as dead now, that will help me in the future.

To address the issue, I reviewed my open reports and culled anyone who had not opened my last three campaigns. I hope that I reduced my list down to the most engaged people...while I still can use open rates to track them. After the iOS update, I'll no longer be able to cull my list based on open rates. I'll just have to keep doing what I'm doing and hope for the best. Sometimes, that's all you can do.

RECENT MARKETING FAILINGS

This is one of those chapters where I talk about lessons I learned this quarter for which I should have known better.

My podcasts were great marketing vehicles. I would come up with an idea, float it on my podcasts to test its viability, and then, when I published the book, I would announce it on my podcasts, my email list, and my YouTube channel.

A nice amount of sales came from my podcasts. Yet, because life is interesting and beautiful, I stopped podcasting, even though I knew it would diminish my sales.

When I released my books *Indie Author Confidential Vol. 5* and *Authors, Steal This Book*, I could only rely on my email list and my YouTube channel. My YouTube audience is not interested in my high-concept books.

I announced the book to my audience in my newsletter, but I know the book would have done better if I had still been podcasting.

This is the negative consequence of living your truth, but I don't regret it for a second.

I made some technical errors in sending out the newsletter. This was because I was so used to relying on my podcasts for much of my marketing exposure. First, Amazon hadn't price-matched the book to free yet, so it was $0.99 on Amazon but free everywhere else. That wasn't a huge deal, but I forgot to include a link to where Amazon readers could download the book for free without paying the $0.99. After all, that would have been the right thing to do.

Several people emailed me asking when the book would be free on Amazon. That's when I knew I'd made a mistake. I had to email my list again with a new link that included a direct download on Book Funnel. It's never a good idea to send your readers two emails in a day. I had a few people unsubscribe because of it. So yeah, that lost me money and engagement. There's always a price for your mistakes.

Even worse, I included the book for free on my website, but I didn't mention that!

Oh, Michael...

That's what happens when you don't send out an email list regularly. You make little mistakes like that, and your communication becomes lackluster because you're not writing email copy regularly. I need to be better about emailing my list monthly, but it got away from me. Now that I have more time, I'll try to do better.

MY GENERAL MARKETING STRATEGY (OR LACK THEREOF)

I've been thinking about marketing lately, though not much. Becoming a world-class marketer is one of my core strategies, yet you would be shocked how little time I spend thinking about marketing. It should probably be a crime.

But even though marketing is a key strategy for me, I'm more interested in marketing my way.

I believe that a writer in today's age has three potential strategies to make money:

Strategy #1 is to write books that target a specific audience and do as much as possible to please them. Sometimes this includes writing to market, but more often than not, it just means writing books that you love that serve a chosen audience. This writer can also create a bonanza with their backlist if they write continuously in one genre.

This strategy maximizes profit in the short term, and if a writer is smart at business, they'll set themselves up nicely for the long term. This strategy may involve writing a lot of books quickly or it may not. It depends on the author.

The first downside of this strategy is burnout. They may get tired of writing the books that make them money. This can lead to the second downside, which is the "golden handcuffs" problem. This writer may wake up one day and decide they don't want to write the books that make them money. They may be unable to do this without losing a substantial amount of their readership.

To summarize the choices in this strategy:

- Write books "in the pocket" of the market.
- Maximize income with every new title and with your backlist.
- Decide whether you want to write at a high volume or whether you want to produce at a slower pace. The faster you write, the more money you make, but the higher your risk of burnout.

Strategy #2 involves writing what you want. You focus less on the market and more on writing the books that make you happy. You write as many books as you can, but only a few will make the majority of your money. The 80/20 rule applies (20 percent of your books will drive 80 percent of your income). This strategy is riskier than the first strategy because you may never find a proper market for your work or build an avid readership. The risk of burnout is the same, but the burnout is different; whereas the first writer burns out over writing books they are no longer passionate about and cannot seem to change direction without destroying the career they built so far, the second writer burns out because they feel that their career will never take off. This strategy sacrifices short-term profit for long-term resiliency. If this author is persistent enough to keep publishing, they may eventually hit a series that does very, very well. If that happens, then readers may be interested in the author's backlist. But only if the backlist has titles in the same genre.

The biggest downside to this strategy is the cost. The author spends a lot of money on titles that may never make it back.

To summarize this strategy:

- Write books you're passionate about.
- Maximize income with a small core of books that make money. The more books you write, the more the core grows.

Strategy #3 is to write a few books as a launchpad for another career, such as public speaking. The majority of marketing comes from social media or a platform such as podcasting.

My strategy is a mixture of #2 and #3. Strategy #1 has never appealed to me.

I write the books I believe in, even though they may not do well. I write a lot of books quickly, and one or two out of ten do better than the rest. I take that money, reinvest it into the business as smartly as I can, and keep writing. It's a very expensive strategy, but I've been fortunate enough that strategy #3 has helped me. Ironically, I don't look for public speaking events—I've only pitched a speech twice in the eight years I've been doing this. I'm lucky that speaking engagements come to me, which helps me grow the business.

I enjoy this path. Early in my career, I thought that strategy #1 was for me. I wanted to write to market but always found myself not doing it and feeling guilty about it. I felt as if there was something wrong with me for not being a more market-focused writer. I saw so many authors making boatloads of money, and wished I could join them. But no matter what I did, I physically, emotionally, and spiritually *could not* bring myself to write books that I didn't believe in. I landed on strategies #2 and #3 by default. Over time, I've learned that it's the perfect path for me.

I don't do anything that makes me uncomfortable with marketing and promotion. My big bet is that by developing an insanely large and high-quality portfolio of books that have stellar packaging, consistent branding, and good content, then whenever I write "the big one," it will pour gasoline on the rest of my catalogue. With my writing books, I've tried to be intentional about positioning them so that if you like one, you'll buy the rest.

With the *Indie Author Confidential* series, my early goal was to create a deep series as early as possible, which is why I started with a quarterly cadence. After two years, I will have eight volumes, which is a crazy number. Even though I'm decreasing the frequency after 2021, it's not hard to imagine this series going on endlessly.

My fiction is a slower burn. I've committed to the urban fantasy genre, and the more I write in it, the more success I'll see eventually. I also have the cyclical nature of the market going for me. For example, I have two series about necromancers. Necromancers aren't "in vogue" right now, but I'm sure there will be a day in the future when they will be. When they are, I'll be ready. Therefore, a large portfolio affords you more interesting opportunities long-term. If you follow strategy #1 and you only write in one genre, and that genre falls out of favor with readers, you will have to wait until those books are back in style, if they're back in style. While strategy #2 carries more risk, it's safer in the long term if you understand the market and how your book fits. I've written several books that were ahead of the market and I reaped the rewards for being early. But, you never know what will work.

Those are my current thoughts on my marketing strategy or lack thereof.

MY MOST RIDICULOUS PITCH EVER (SERIOUSLY)

I received an invitation to speak at a writing event that paid well. I had a short turnaround time to give an answer and a pitch for a topic.

It was 6:45 AM, and I had to log in to work at 7:30 AM. After work, I had to get ready for a family vacation. If I didn't come up with a pitch in 45 minutes, it wasn't going to happen.

I was half-asleep and needed to come up with something fast.

I came up with the following idea.

Title: Writing App Speed-Dating

Is your current writing app "the one" or are you ready to find another? With so many writing apps on the market, it's hard to choose the best one! In this session, writer Michael La Ronn will demo the hottest writing apps for writers in 2021 and show you their top features. Discover cutting-edge advancements in outlining, writing, and book formatting. After this session, you just might find the writing app you'll want to spend the rest of your writing career with. Featured apps include Atticus, Scrivener, Ulysses, Dabble, and more!

I sent the pitch at 7:25 AM with time to spare! And trust me, I was laughing the entire time.

Funny enough, I wrote the following in this chapter before I heard back from the venue:

Whether the pitch lands me a deal or not, I'm proud that I could pull out copy in such a short time. If I land the event, I'll refine the copy, as I think it could be better, but I think the "spirit" was there.

There is such a thing as too clever copy. If the idea fails, that will probably be the reason. But if it succeeds, then it'll probably be because I went right up to the line between "good" and "clever," but I didn't cross it.

After writing that, I heard back from the venue. It turns out that I landed the event!

Wow—just wow. Sometimes you never know what will work. The pitch was accepted as-is with only a minor modification. While I can't announce the venue just yet, it's definitely a big one—and in-person!

USE A REVIEW IMAGE FOR MARKETING

I worked with a designer on Fiverr who engaged in a marketing tactic I had never seen before.

He designed a set of icons for me. He sent me a photo of all the icons against a blue background and asked that I post the image in my review so others could see the quality of his work.

It was such a great idea that I wondered why no one on Fiverr asked me to do that before.

I thought about adapting this for my writing business but couldn't think of a good way. My initial thought was to ask reviewers to include quotes from the book but I decided against that.

Still, it's such an intriguing idea that I'm capturing it here in case I develop a need for it.

To whatever extent you can control the marketing first impression without violating ethics, asking readers to share something you've prepared that they enjoyed and benefited from is a smart idea.

MEETING A READER UNEXPECTEDLY

A receptionist at a place I frequent surprised me by pulling out a copy of *Be a Writing Machine*, asking me to sign it.

I was humbled. It is always surreal to see my books in the wild. This is why you should publish your book in paperback. You never know when events like this will happen.

Also, this is another reason why you should update your email signature to include a link to your books and a mention that you're an author. That's how this reader learned about my books because I had to email the company a few times. I've been including my author info in my email signature for years, and every once in a while, I see proof that my email signature is working, selling books for me while I sleep. You never know when people will click your signature and buy something. They might even recommend your books to their friends. Just make sure the signature isn't obnoxious. You want it to intrigue people enough to click. Then what happens is up to them.

LETTING MY READERS VOTE ON MY NEXT WORK

I pulled out my early career playbook and used one of my successful strategies.

For my Beast Mode 2021 challenge, I came up with four ideas for writing books. I only had a vague concept of the content.

I asked my patrons on Patreon to vote on which one I should have written first.

The ideas were:

- 250+ Writing Tips, Vol. 3
- Dictation for Writers
- Strategy for Authors
- The Writer's Guide to Writing Apps

My patrons wanted me to write The Writer's Guide to Writing Apps idea, which surprised me.

When I finished that book, I opened the voting up to my community. Once I passed the 75 percent mark of the book I was working on, I opened up a poll that contained all of my ideas, and I wrote whichever book won the majority of the vote. If there was a tie, I broke it with my preference.

When it was time to release my Beast Mode Collection at the end of the quarter, I knew that it would contain the ideas my readers most wanted to read. I also believe this project was good for the long-term profitability of my portfolio because the books I wrote during Beast Mode were proven concepts that connected with hundreds of my readers.

DESIGNING COVERS FOR THE INDIE AUTHOR CONFIDENTIAL SERIES

When I launched my *Indie Author Confidential* series in 2020, I treated it as a separate brand. I wanted the book covers to look familiar to readers who read my flagship writing books, but I also wanted the books to have their own style.

I worked with my nonfiction cover designer to create a new brand. I found some images on royalty-free sites that I liked; black vector objects with a door opening within them. They had a mysterious look, as if a secret were behind the door.

I found a group of images by the same designer: a lock, a puzzle piece, a book, a heart, and a keyhole. These were the images for the first five books of this series.

Then there were no more.

I wanted to continue with this aesthetic, so I hired an illustrator, sent him the images for the first five books, and told them to design objects in the same style:

- Typewriter
- Pencil
- Dollar sign
- Safe

- e-reader/tablet
- Chess piece
- Coffee cup
- Notebook
- Light bulb

Overall, I paid the illustrator about $150. It was an easy job for him. I paid higher than what most people pay for this type of service because I wanted good work.

Now I have images I can send to my designer to continue the same look for the series. I have enough images to last me a few years.

PRICING PSYCHOLOGY

When I wrote *Authors, Steal This Book*, I struggled with how many ideas to include in the book. I like including numbers in book titles and subtitles because they signal value.

I knew that I would include every idea from the first five volumes of the *Indie Author Confidential* series, but I didn't want that number to be awkward (like 69).

I started with 64 ideas. Was that the right number? I did some basic research on number psychology, and I found some interesting opinions. I didn't verify whether scientific data supports these assertions, but they are at least thought-provoking.

The number one signifies a beginning.

Odd numbers are considered to be masculine and even numbers are feminine.

Seven is a lucky number. In Judaism and Christianity, God created the world in seven days. There are seven continents on Earth. Pricing that ends in seven just works for mysterious reasons.

Ten is considered to be a practical number and a "complete" number. Eleven is one more than ten, so it is above and beyond.

Thirteen is unlucky.

But what about 64?

According to Google, six means harmony. Four means the number of justice.

Justice? Nah. That didn't match the theme of the book.

What about 67? According to Google (emphasis is mine), "The essence of the number 67 is focused on family and home issues and *providing a long-lasting security for the future.* The number 67 in numerology also signifies foundation, focus, family, *idealism, introspection, and pragmatism...*"

I could have picked 68, which is also an idealistic number, but I liked a number ending in seven. I wrote three extra ideas so I could hit 67, and voila! That's how I arrived at the right number.

PRICE DROP FOR THE INDIE AUTHOR CONFIDENTIAL SERIES

I have now published six volumes of *Indie Author Confidential*. I decided it was time to use a new marketing tactic: dropping the price of the first book to make it a loss leader. I dropped Volume 1 from $4.99 to $2.99, which is a 40-percent decrease.

I include Volumes 1 through 3 in an omnibus edition. That costs $9.99. When each of the volumes was $4.99, the true value of that collection was $14.97. When I dropped the price of Volume 1, the true value also dropped slightly to $12.97, which is still a good deal, given that it sells for $9.99.

At the end of 2021, I'll be creating a second omnibus that contains Volumes 4 through 7. When that happens, I may drop the price of the first omnibus so that it is a slightly better deal.

When I have so many volumes, I can afford to lose a couple of dollars on the first volume.

I plan on continuing this series as long as possible, so I will continue to refine the pricing of the individual volumes and omnibuses as the years progress. One day, if I have 30 or 40 volumes available, this may well be the most valuable piece of intellectual property that I own, especially if I become a popular bestseller and a full-time author. At speaking events, I'll be able to point people to a gigantic series that has all my secrets.

AN UPDATE ON MY PERMAFREE SITUATION

I mentioned that I made *Authors, Steal This Book* permafree. It's the first writing book I've ever made free. I figured it would be an interesting experiment.

Permafree is a slow burn. The last time I did this was in 2015 with my book *Android Paradox*. That book did extremely well as a permafree title, with tens of thousands of downloads and a healthy number of sales for books two and three.

When I published the book, I was able to set it to free on every retailer except Amazon, since Amazon doesn't allow free pricing. However, Amazon will price-match your book from another retailer if it's free there.

Amazon must follow Apple's pricing because it did not price-match the book until it was for sale on Apple for 48 hours. Apple had a significant delay in publishing my book for some reason.

Once the book was free, it racked up a couple of dozen downloads a week. I pushed some Amazon Ads to it and that improved the number somewhat. At the time of this writing, it didn't have any reviews.

I didn't expect anything crazy to happen with the book, and so far, nothing has. But it's good to know that permafree is still a viable strategy in getting a book to readers.

WHAT'S YOUR DEFICIENCY?

I needed my gutters cleaned. I have a contractor that I normally hire, but he didn't return my calls. I gave him three weeks, and nothing.

I went online to find an alternative company. Almost none of them called me back. A few did, and what ensued was a pathetic parade of contractors.

One guy charged me four times what I typically pay. I declined him outright.

Another said he was backed up for several months. Declined.

And then, I called a final gutter cleaning company and seemingly tripped into another universe.

First, the website was odd. They were a gutter-cleaning service in my area, but the website looked like a marketing scam. I'm making the following text up, but hopefully, you can see why I was suspicious: "Gutter Cleaning Des Moines. The countrywide gutter cleaners. Call 1-800..." There were also several hundred 5-star reviews from customers on the website, but if you looked up the site on other websites, it had 1- and 2-star reviews.

A local contractor with a 1-800 number. That never turns out well.

I'm picky about contractors, but I was pretty much desperate at this point, and if I didn't do something, I'd have water issues around my foundation. I called the 1-800 number, and someone answered who wasn't from my area. She wasn't from Des Moines because of the way she said the name (It's pronounced "Duh moyn," but out-of-towners always say "Duh-moyns." It's a dead giveaway.) I don't think she was in the United States either, but you never really know.

The representative was very professional and took my address, asked me a few questions, and gave me a quote over the phone. She told me to expect a phone call within 7 days when the contractor would be on the way. Payment would be facilitated by email.

So far, so good.

I got a confirmation email that confirmed the price, deadline for the work to be completed by, and a courtesy notice of which credit cards they accepted.

We had several days of thunderstorms, and she even called me to let me know that they had to reschedule. She gave me a new deadline. Very, very professional.

Yet, the entire experience was giving me anxiety. On the day the cleaning was scheduled, I thought, "This is either going to be excellent, or it's going to be a dumpster fire." I had no idea who the hell was liable to show up at my doorstep.

I received a phone call at 11:30 AM from a guy who told me he was on the way. He was friendly and pleasant. When he arrived, it was in a giant, unmarked van with two ladders strapped to the top. The guy was careful and even rinsed off a mess he made on my driveway.

He did a phenomenal job. As soon as he left, I received an email with an invoice and I paid it.

That's not how I expected this to end. I paid a little more for the service, but I got what I paid for.

I kept waiting for the "gotcha." Afterward, I searched again to see if this company was a scam or a front for a burglary operation. But no, it turns out that they were legit after all.

It got me thinking about how every business is a radar chart between speed, quality, and price. My first boss taught me that. Customers can only choose two of the three.

- They can get a high-quality experience for cheap, but it will take a long time.
- They can get a cheap experience very quickly, but the quality will be average.
- They can get fast service with quality, but it will expensive.

I'd say the gutter experience was quick, cheap, and above-average quality. That's incredibly rare. This company defied the laws of business, which is why I was fascinated by the exchange.

That got me thinking about the business of writing. Now I don't think it is fair to say that readers should only be entitled to two out of the three attributes. They deserve all three. But every writer has their deficiencies.

To frame this better, let's say that the real attributes are craft, business, and marketing. Every writer is good at two.

As for me, I learn craft quickly and I have a business sense for publishing. Marketing will always be my deficiency.

Other writers I know are phenomenal marketers and amazing craftspeople, but they're terrible at business. Others are good at business and marketing, but their writing skills need serious work. Some writers excel at all three, but they are rare, just like the gutter-cleaning business I hired.

I challenge you to consider these strengths and weaknesses whenever you discover a new author.

As a writer, what are your deficiencies?

BECOME A TECHNOLOGY AND DATA-DRIVEN WRITER

TWO BOOKS IN ONE

I was watching a YouTube video about finance and accounting. I watched a boring video about life insurance, but at the end, the YouTuber pulled out a book and said, "If you want to learn more about the strategies I've used to build wealth, I've got a book for you. It's called X and I've written it two ways. The first way is for the data-minded, but if that's not your thing, just flip it over and I give you the same information in story format."

My head exploded. After I got over my initial shock of what an *amazing* idea this was, I tried to figure out how the heck he did it.

I thought, "Surely, Amazon's Kindle Direct Publishing program would never allow this." And I was right. Their website says, "All pages and content must be oriented the same way. Pages can contain some upside-down text as long as the rest of the page contents are right side up (e.g., a book of riddles with answers printed upside-down on the page)."

Maybe Ingram Spark allows this. I doubt it, but I couldn't find anything on their website about it. I think you'd have to hire an offset printer, honestly.

Technically, I stepped through how one could accomplish this feature:

- You'd need a print cover that had two front covers. You'd have to have one cover for Book A, a regular spine, and then another cover for Book B. The second cover would have to be upside-down.
- From front to back, the text for Book A would need to be right-side-up, but the text for Book B would need to be upside-down and in reverse order. You would need a clean delineation within the interior so that readers wouldn't get confused.
- The "middle ground" of the book poses an interesting design and usability opportunity; you could use some sort of page design on the edges of the page to indicate where both books end.
- The page numbers, headers, and footers for Book B would also need to upside-down and in reverse order.

I'm intrigued by the idea. That said, it'd be difficult for a self-published author to pull off. But if they did, there would be unique use cases:

- A two-sided novel, with one book told from the perspective of the hero and another told from the perspective of the villain. (Or, two characters of the author's choosing.)
- An "A/B" novel, with the first half being the novel in its original format and the second being an "author's cut" with extra scenes.
- A "what if" novel with the first book being the original novel as the author intended, and then a

"what if" novel where it branches down a different path around the middle, with an alternative ending.

- A two-sided self-help book, with the first book written for analytical people and the second book written for creatives.
- A double feature, with a novel from two different but complementary authors as a cross-promotional tactic. This could also be done with nonfiction and poetry.

There are lots of opportunities with an idea like this. Maybe one day it'll be easier for indies to pull off.

SECONDHAND BOOK SALES:
ANOTHER REASON TO BUY ISBNS?

I encountered an article in *The Guardian* about an effort underway in the United Kingdom to pay authors for second-hand sales of their books.

In international copyright law, the "first sale doctrine" has always dictated that authors can make money on the first sale of their book but not subsequent sales. This keeps used book sales in demand and makes it easier for books to be sold without having to worry about licensing.

I have mixed feelings about the first sale doctrine; on the one hand, I would love the ability to make money off second-hand sales, but on the other hand, I also understand that whether I make money directly from them or not, I still make money. Readers who buy a used book and love it will go on to explore more of the author's backlist, and maybe even buy books on the frontlist too. It's possible that putting an additional burden on used bookstores could reduce book sales for authors across the board, so I suppose we have to be careful what we wish for.

In the UK initiative, two used booksellers partnered to create a royalty fund for authors whose books are sold secondhand. With each sale, the retailers contribute to the fund. Each author receives a payout of up to £1,000 (which is approximately $1,400 USD at the time of this writing). The payments are facilitated through the Authors' Licensing and Collection Society (ALCS) in the UK.

Here's how the ALCS describes themselves on their about page: "We make sure you receive the money you're entitled to as a writer when someone copies or uses your work. We collect money from all over the world, then pay it to our members. So far we've paid a total of £570 million."

Authors pay a £36-lifetime membership fee. ALCS puts the author in a database, and if they find a match on dues owed as a result of a mass licensing deal or another project, they pass the money along to the author after taking a 9.5 percent commission. Anyone in the world can join, and I presume that this includes indie authors since they are not excluded in their eligibility guidelines.

Back to the subject of this article, I have some concerns. £1,000 is merely a token amount after taxes and the ALCS's commission. Also, I doubt something like this would ever happen globally, though it would be nice. US retailers are in too dire straits to do something like this.

However, this paragraph grabbed my attention (emphasis is mine):

"*Participating retailers will share their sales information with the ALCS,* which will match the works with their writer members and pay them their royalties as a lump sum twice a year."

Let's say that something like this *did* go global. How would retailers facilitate payment? This is predominantly a data concern.

Book retailers would probably collect sales data based on ISBNs. If a secondhand book doesn't have an ISBN, it technically won't exist and that book's author won't be covered in the fund. Hence, if an author wants to participate in a program like this, they would need to use ISBNs. Otherwise, the fund gets to keep that money, which means it earns interest and can be invested.

If something like this were to happen in the US, then ISBNs would be required to participate. This would be yet another reason to invest in ISBNs...if it happened!

But again, let's do some math. Even if my books were sold secondhand, which I imagine that they are, I'd have to sell a lot to reach the $1,400 cap. But even if I did, I'd have to account for taxes.

How much do ISBNs cost in the US? $575 for a pack of 500 and $1,500 for a pack of 1,000.

Still not worth the money.

ATTICUS: THE APP I PREDICTED

In Volume 2 of this series, I laid out my vision of the writing app of the future. I'm reposting the article here in its entirety because I am going to brag at the end.

▭

The writer of the future needs a unified command center. Not a writing app, a formatting app, a spelling and grammar app, and the myriad other software we use.

My workflow today is as follows: I write my books in Scrivener, then export them to Microsoft Word so that my editor can edit using track changes. I review the editor's edits in Microsoft Word, run the manuscript through ProWritingAid, copy/paste the book back into Scrivener, then export to Vellum for formatting.

I despise the workflow, but it's the best we have right now.

It's unreasonable to expect one app to execute on the level of Scrivener, Microsoft Word, ProWritingAid, *and* Vellum, but it is reasonable to ask that the writing apps of the future work together seamlessly.

I'd like to write my novel in Scrivener and be able to send it to my editor, perhaps by granting the editor permission to edit my Scrivener file with tracked changes (if Scrivener ever supports that). Preferably, I should never have to leave my writing app for anything, even formatting.

The bestselling writing apps on the market are extremely vulnerable for disruption. Writers just don't realize it because the writing app as we know it hasn't changed in forty years and we can't conceive of how it can possibly evolve.

If a new writing app functioned similar to how I describe the following narrative, it would render the current landscape of writing apps irrelevant. Let's call it Shapeshifter.

Shapeshifter is a writing app that offers an interchangeable interface that supports WYSIWIG (what you see is what you get) writing interface a la Microsoft Word, or a markdown experience like Ulysses. With one click, you can change its appearance and therefore its layout. It's two or three different writing apps in one. That's the app's headlining feature. It "shapeshifts" extremely well, molding itself to suit the writer instead of asking the writer to adapt to it.

The desktop version is available on Windows and Linux. Mac users were originally left out, but they quickly learned that they could run the app by installing Windows on their computers—a deliberate and intelligent choice on the developers' part that allowed them to seize the Windows market, which was ripe for a new, modern competitor. Given the benefits you're about to hear, Mac users will have no qualms about upgrading their computers to quickly abandon their current writing app. Ironically, the app is available on iOS, iPad OS, and Android, with good feature parity so that users can write on-the-go no matter their phone or tablet.

Shapeshifter is also available in the browser, with an optimized writing experience.

No matter where you are or what device you are using, Shapeshifter will shift to suit your preference.

If that were it, Shapeshifter would be remarkable. But here's what makes it the writing app of the future: out of the box, the app itself is not terribly robust. It has a few key features such as a word processor and the ability to import and export.

However, the app has way more features available; you purchase what you need. If you don't need a distraction-free mode, you don't have to pay for it. If you ever want it, you pay a one-time fee of $5. The app and its features are like LEGOs that you can snap together based on your preferences. Every writer's app will look different; in fact, writers are encouraged to share their "space," which is linked to a generous affiliate program that rewards them for every referral they make.

Shapeshifter is also the first writing app other than Microsoft Word to offer third-party developer integration. The app's in-house features are comparable to most other writing apps, and without any integrations, it looks rather vanilla. Third-party integrations are where the app shines. Developers can create new kinds of writing tools—outlining features, dictation support, macros, and integration with other apps, like voice assistants. All of these plugins help you become a better version of yourself. This also allows the app to stay on at the forefront of advancements in operating systems.

Shapeshifter offers a Discord or a Reddit community where users can request new plugins and developers can create them. The app gathers a cult following that quickly becomes mainstream.

Now, let's talk about the biggest selling point: the price.

Shapeshifter's developers wanted to create an affordable writing app and avoid the ire of the community by switching pricing models. For a one-time fee of $30, you pay to own the app. The developers keep the prices low because you pay a la carte for additional features such as cloud syncing between mobile and desktop and WordPress blog integration, for example. You only pay for the features you'll actually use. Overall, you might pay around $200-300 over the lifetime of the app, more including plugins, which can range from a couple dollars to a few hundred dollars depending on the plugin.

And that's not all...

Shapeshifter is just one app in a suite of apps for writers. Shapeshifter Writer handles the writing. You see, the developers figured out that it's impossible to do everything well in one app, so they modeled their app suite after the Adobe Creative Cloud so that all their apps work together seamlessly.

Shapeshifter Writer is an app and marketplace for *writing*.

When it's time to edit, the writer can, with the click of a button, "shift" the app into Editor mode, which is technically a separate application in its own right that you can also purchase.

Editor is optimized for editing. Shapeshifter Editor is a pioneering editing app that is designed solely for back-and-forth between a writer and editor. Drawing inspiration from apps like Google Docs and Asana, a writer and editor can collaborate on a manuscript without the manuscript ever leaving the Editor ecosystem. All the author has to do is invite the editor to join a given project. The editor can edit the book in a browser and does not need to purchase the software, though doing so under an Editor's license will grant them unique benefits.

All edits that the author accepts in Editor get pushed to Writer so that the manuscript is in sync everywhere. The author can of course revert and rollback changes at any time.

Editor also supports third-party integration, such as Grammarly, ProWritingAid, and anything else a developer can dream of in the editing process. Editor would also encourage and support artificial intelligence plugins.

When it's time to format your manuscript, you can "shift" to

Shapeshifter Formatter with the click of a button. With just one click and a smooth wizard, you can have a publish-ready ebook and print edition. It offers the power of Vellum but also third-party integration for formatting templates and special features such as indexes. You could even grant access to a formatter who could upload HTML that the app would accept. Changes you make in Formatter are automatically synced with Writer and Editor.

Formatter even integrates with book retailer APIs so you can publish without having to leave the app.

Shapeshifter's holy triumvirate of Writer, Editor, and Formatter succeeds because it streamlines the process of writing and helps writers do more in less time. It takes advantage of the fact that some writing apps go years without receiving updates as well as writers' frustration with subscription-based apps. It leverages the power of Adobe-smooth integration between the three apps, with the ease of use and customization of Reaper (a very popular sound recording app among musicians).

While the future of writing apps may look different than the narrative I've written, consider that writing apps as we know them haven't changed much in forty years as I mentioned earlier. With emerging technology, writers will have such a need to evolve that it will be a no-brainer if someone offers them the ability to move to the cutting edge of technology and writing.

━━

I wrote Volume 2 of this series between July and September of 2020.

Here we are in July 2021, and now we have an app called Atticus, created by Dave Chesson of Kindlepreneur fame. Atticus is still in beta at the time of this writing. Dave is one of the brightest tech minds in publishing, and I don't say that lightly.

I have no idea if Dave read Volume I of this series. I'm willing to bet he didn't. Yet, consider Atticus's feature set:

- It is a web-based writing app that (in the future) will allow you to use it on any device.
- It has a writing mode that rivals most top-tier writing apps.
- It has a formatting mode that matches much of Vellum's functionality, including paperback formatting.
- In the future, it will support an editing mode where your editor can edit your book within the app itself. You just give them a link and the necessary permissions.

Wow. It happened just like that: we are now looking at the writing app of the future. While it doesn't have ALL the features I mentioned, it has the most important ones.

If Atticus takes off, it will rapidly erode Scrivener's market share. Scrivener's biggest weakness is that you cannot edit your book effectively within it; most people export to Microsoft Word or Google Docs and work with their editor there. Then they import the work back into Scrivener, or into a separate formatting app like Vellum. Scrivener also does not excel at book formatting. It is possible to create good-looking ebooks with it, but not paperbacks.

If Atticus can pull off the "one-stop shopping" approach by offering a single ecosystem that the book never has to leave, the entire field of writing apps will have to play catch-up. Some will never catch up.

Will I migrate to Atticus? Not yet. When the following things happen, I will consider it:

- I want assurances that my data is protected in the browser, with the ability to back it up to another source in case of a hacking attempt.
- I want the ability to write on my phone with the same ease as Scrivener and Ulysses iOS. Atticus currently functions as a progressive web app on iOS, but that's not good enough for my needs.
- The editing mode needs to work smoothly and eliminates back and forth within Microsoft Word between my editor and me (and my editor has to rave about it).

Atticus is the writing app to watch. It has a special blend of features that can change the writing process as we know it.

THOUGHTS ON ARCHIVING DATA

Every few years, I reflect on my data archiving strategy. Data changes with the times, and if you're not careful, you'll lose your data.

(When I refer to data, I'm talking about your books. Your books are data, but most people don't think of them that way.)

I was cleaning out my basement and stumbled upon some physical photographs that I had taken long, long ago with a disposable camera. I used to buy disposables at my local drug store for $10, take 30 photos, have them developed at a photo lab, and then receive a pouch with 30 photos and a roll of negatives. It's amazing how far camera technology has come.

How do you archive those old disposable photos? The photo quality degrades over time unless you protect them in an album. It's probably best to digitize them. But how do you do that? You buy a scanner and upload them to your computer in the highest quality possible.

Once the photos have made the migration to your computer, how do you ensure that they outlive your computer? Most people either use digital hard drives or cloud services. What happens when those hard drives fail in five years, or the cloud service gets acquired or goes out of business? If you care about your data, you're always engaged in a constant battle to keep it available and preserved.

The same is true with our books. Have you thought about what data standards will be popular in 2041? I think about it all the time.

Today, writers currently use some combination of the below formats:

- Microsoft Word .DOC or .DOCX
- Rich text file (.RTF)
- OpenOffice (.ODT)
- A proprietary format such as Scrivener (.SCRIV), which is a bundle of .RTF files
- Plain text (.TXT)
- Portable Digital File (.PDF)
- Electronic Publication Format (.EPUB)
- MOBI Pocket (.MOBI)
- Google Docs format

Let's examine each format, its strengths and weaknesses, and the challenges that will exist in 2041.

Microsoft Word. It's hard to argue that Microsoft Word *won't* be around in 2041. It is the program of choice for just about every profession when it comes to writing letters and correspondence. But what if political winds shift against Microsoft (as they did in the nineties)? In the next section, I write about a potential antitrust problem brewing in the tech sector, and that could affect Microsoft. What if Moore's Law becomes true and the processing power of computer chips stops doubling every two years? What if Silicon Valley, a shining beacon in the tech world today, becomes a rust belt and an economically depressed region? (Yes, I know Microsoft, along with Amazon, is located in Washington, but follow along.) If Silicon Valley goes the way of department stores such as Sears and JC Penney, then it's not unreasonable to think that Microsoft could sell assets that don't perform. It's also possible that a competitor could release a new technology that renders Word obsolete and irrelevant. Of course, these events may not happen. More practically, though, it's certainly possible that Microsoft will *at least* update the Word format between now and 2041, just like they did when they created the .DOCX format. That means that .DOCX will likely become obsolete in the future.

Rich Text File. This format was also created by Microsoft in 1987 as a way to create cross-compatibility between Windows and Macintosh versions of Microsoft Word. Microsoft discontinued it in 2008 but it is still widely used.

Just by its association with Microsoft, I'd put RTF in the same category of concern as .DOCX.

OpenOffice. I'm not too familiar with the OpenOffice format, but I know it's popular among writers who can't afford (or use) Microsoft Word. OpenOffice is open-source software, so there's always a chance that people in the community will stop supporting it in favor of a new format.

Proprietary formats. Will Scrivener be around in 2041? I hope so, but it's a safe bet to *assume* it won't. There-fore, if the .SCRIV format is the only way you're backing up your work (which is just a bunch of .RTF files), you're asking for trouble in about twenty years. I hope Scrivener will continue to flourish, but Literature & Latte is a small busi-ness, and small businesses fall on hard times. Its founder won't be around forever, and who knows what will happen after that? Scrivener could get acquired or discontinued. And once that happens, it's anyone's guess. I believe that it's a smart strategy to export *all* contents of your Scrivener binder to formats that exist outside of your Scrivener file. This includes:

- Research
- Outlines
- Manuscript
- Any other materials used in the creation of your manuscript

Save those files separately in addition to your .SCRIV file. This way, if you wake up one morning and Scrivener is gone, your work will persist. Don't be one of the writers who say "that will never happen" and then find themselves scrambling.

Oh, and this also applies to Vellum. Just because Vellum is doing well now doesn't mean it will in 2041.

This applies to *any* writing app. I'm just singling out Scrivener and Vellum because they're the most prominent right now.

(Much love and respect to the people at Literature & Latte and 180g, but I'm being a realist. No one is immune to the inevitable tide of life and death.)

Plain text. If there's one format that is sure to be around in 2041, it's plain text. It's a universal format. That said, it's not helpful for working with books. If you back up your work in plain text, I hope you'll never need it, because you'll have to do a lot of work to reproduce your book in the format that you intended.

PDFs. I believe PDFs will still be around in 2041, but they might be a legacy format. Saving your book as a PDF is required anyway if you publish paperbacks, so most authors are already using this format. An issue with PDFs used to be character recognition—if the PDF you used didn't allow for text manipulation, you couldn't convert it without using some type of optical character recognition (OCR) software. Authors don't have that problem.

ePUB and MOBI. ePUB and MOBI are the predominant ebook formats. Will ePUBs be around in 2041? I think so. Amazon discontinued support for the .MOBI format for new titles in 2021, though it is still accepted and read by Kindle devices. An ePUB is just a bunch of HTML files, and I don't see HTML going anywhere any time soon. This is good news for authors. ePUB is probably the most reliable format we'll have moving forward, assuming that nothing bad happens to Microsoft.

Google Docs. Google will never kill Google Docs, right? Right? Consider the website Killed by Google, which is a graveyard of all the projects Google has scrapped. Google doesn't care if a product is popular; it has its own reasons for ending projects, and it ends them all the time. While I'm optimistic about the future of Google Docs, I don't forget for a second that Google is capable of killing projects in a moment's notice. That makes Google Docs less reliable, and I would not include Google Docs in my long-term data preservation strategy.

Am I an alarmist? I hope not. I'm just trying to be real about the advancement of technology.

It's not enough to think about the data. You also have to think about how it will be stored.

No one stores their data on floppy disks anymore, and almost no one uses CDs or DVDs for data storage either.

What about external hard drives? The research I've done suggests that rotations per minute (RPM) drives may be the most reliable, but they still fail and break down like any other hard drive. I've also seen people argue that solid-state drives (SSD) aren't much better. And regardless of which one is "better," is there any guarantee that computers will contain them or be able to read them in 2041 ? Of course not! After all, how many new computers have CD and DVD drives in 2021? None! Ah, technology...

There is no clear answer here except to update your external hard drives every three to five years and migrate your data to the new devices to account for new advancements in technology.

After this exercise, I refined my data preservation strategy.

1. I save all my books in .SCRIV, .DOCX, .RTF, .EPUB, and .PDF. I'm already doing this today.
2. I store all my books on my computer, in the cloud, on an external hard drive, on external USB "thumb" drives, and on an automatic backup service.
3. I update my external hard drives every three to five years.

I spent a Sunday afternoon reviewing my book files and filling in any gaps. I forgot to save one series as an .RTF, for example. I also never exported my outlines, research, and so on. That's all done now, and backed up across all my different backup locations.

That's all I can do. I'm confident in knowing that no matter what happens in the future with file formats and storage technology, I'll see it coming before others, and I'll be able to make the migration without too much difficulty.

BACKUP BEST PRACTICES WEBINAR

I attended a webinar sponsored by Backblaze, the company I use for automatic data backups. I highly recommend Backblaze because they saved my data when my other backup sources failed a few years ago. It is my safety net—I never hope I have to use it, but when I do, I'm glad I had it.

The webinar was called "State of Backups 2021" and I learned some new concepts that I wanted to memorialize here because the Backblaze team said the same things I've been saying on my platforms for years. If anyone knows about how to protect your data, it's Backblaze.

Here were the takeaways.

- They did a study with a data firm and did a broad sampling of people across the United States. They asked them about their backup habits. Only 11 percent of participants backed up their work.
- Eleven percent of participants backed up their work weekly, 11 percent backed up their data monthly, 58 percent of people did it yearly or every few years, and 20 percent *never* backed up their work.

- Sixty-two percent of participants have lost data at some point, 76 percent deleted something by accident, 51 percent have had an internal or external hard drive crash, and 61 percent had a security incident such as ransomware or a virus. Twenty-five percent of those incidents happened within the last year.
- They did a "best backup persona" of the ideal person who exercises best practices based on their sampling. That persona is a female 35 to 44 years old.
- They explained the difference between cloud syncing and true backup. Cloud syncing (used by services such as Dropbox, Google Drive, and iCloud) merely makes sure that your files are the most up-to-date versions. The cloud keeps everything current. True backup saves every version of your work (naturally, Backblaze offers true backup).
- They recommended the 3-2-1 backup method, which means saving *at least* three copies of your files, with two copies kept onsite in your home (i.e., on your computer and external hard drive) and at least one off-site (using a service like Backblaze or with a bank safety deposit box).
- They recommended testing your backups regularly. The worst time to figure out if your backups work is when something happens. Test your backups regularly so that you'll know how to use them in a crisis.
- If a ransomware attack happens, kiss your files in the cloud goodbye; the software may corrupt or infect the most up-to-date files without a way for

you to restore older versions (in most cases; some cloud services do support limited versioning). True backup can protect you against ransomware because even if an attack locks your computer down, the bad guys can't access older versions of your files. Just log in to your backup service from a secure location, select your last backup, and download it. (See why backing up multiple times a day is smart?) They'll even ship you a hard drive with your data if needed.

It was a great webinar and I hope participants learned how to protect their data better.

To distill these best practices down so that you become a "best backup persona" (with some added tips of my own):

- Invest in a backup service that backs up your work *at least* daily, but hopefully more. Backblaze can do this for you, but there are other competitors such as Carbonite that do the same thing.
- Use cloud services for the syncing benefits they offer, but don't expect them to save you.
- Learn how to spot phishing attempts. Many computer compromises happen because someone clicks on an attachment in an email.
- Be careful when browsing the Internet and visiting sites you're unfamiliar with. If you get hit with a ransomware attack or debilitating virus, it might happen while you're researching your book or when you're troubleshooting a computer problem. Be extraordinarily careful these days when you're researching your books.
- Use the 3-2-1 backup method.

- Develop a written plan for ransomware attacks. They're on the rise. I've been talking about them since 2019, and unfortunately, I was correct in predicting that they would start hitting average consumers (and writers) more frequently. A sound ransomware strategy will detail what to do to recover your data, diagnose the problem, and what to do with the infected computer. If you do your job correctly, you won't have to pay the ransom because you'll never lose your data. Start planning now.
- Follow these best practices, and you'll never lose your data. If you do, you'll severely minimize the amount of data you lose. Whether it be a ransomware attack or an honest mistake that deletes your manuscript permanently from your computer, you'll be protected.

I'll keep talking about this until people listen.

WIRELESS HARD DRIVES

As I mentioned in the previous chapter, it has been approximately three years since I upgraded my external hard drives, so this year, I was in the market for new ones.

I was pleased to see that wireless hard drives have become more affordable. The disk emits its own Wi-Fi network. You can plug them into your computer or transmit files to it via Wi-Fi. This comes with its own problems—namely, it's one more thing that can go wrong in the hardware—but it's a convenient feature.

I have limited desk space, and new computers come with fewer and fewer USB ports these days. Being able to transmit my files to a hard drive wirelessly is a godsend. Also, as a security measure, I can turn the hard drive's wireless functionality on and off, which helps prevent access to it in a hacking event.

I always buy external hard drives in groups of two because they can and do fail. For Amazon Prime Day, I got a great deal on two drives: a SanDisk 32GB Connect Wireless Stick Flash Drive and a Samsung Portable T5 SSD drive.

The Samsung SSD drive will be plugged into my computer all the time. It will take over when my current hard drive fails, which will be any day now, as it has been acting funny. The SanDisk will not be plugged into my computer. It will be my wireless backup, but I will only turn on the wireless functionality when I'm backing up my work. Otherwise, it will be turned off for security purposes.

Investing in both hard drives cost me approximately $200, but it was money well-spent to protect my work and preserve it for the future.

MY EXPERIENCE WITH COWORKING
SPACES

I took a new job last quarter as an insurance executive, and the job is 100 percent work from home.

Before the pandemic, I worked from home one or two days a week already, so I had an easier transition into the new lifestyle. When you're working from home, certain amenities that you take for granted in an office setting can be detrimental in your home environment if they stop working. Of course, I'm referring to the Internet!

If your Internet goes out when you're working from home, you're screwed. All you can do is get down on your knees, pray, and then hope it comes back on as quickly as possible. If that doesn't work, you have to call your Internet service provider. By that point, your absence may be noticed by your employer, especially if your Internet went out during an important conference call. (As is the case with me. My Internet *always* goes out during an important conference call when I'm the one leading the meeting.)

Internet outages are unacceptable. Sure, they happen. When you work from home but your employer has an office nearby, employers understand this and will often accommodate you by offering you a desk to work at while your outage gets resolved. But the nearest office my employer owns is six hours away in Chicago...

When you work from home and your Internet goes out, you have to make choices quickly. If the outage is for a few minutes, or even an hour, you can make up the time. Hopefully, you have a boss who understands (and even better, they're experiencing the outage too!) If the outage is longer or you have a boss that is less lenient, you have to use your paid time off (and in the United States, we don't get much PTO, even though we over-work ourselves). If you don't have any time to use, you will get fired. For this reason, my Internet presence needs to be up and operational 99.99 percent of the time, 24 hours a day, 7 days a week. I'm not getting fired because of a public utility's incompetence.

I wrote in a previous volume about how I invested in Ethernet ports in my home so I could use a hardwire Internet connection for my podcast interviews and work calls. That worked extremely well and almost completely eliminated my Internet issues.

However, I also made another contingency plan. What would I do if my neighborhood suffered a power outage? In August 2020, a derecho blew through Iowa and most of the state lost power for at least a week. If a mass Internet outage happened again, what would I do?

I signed up with a local coworking space to rent office space on an as-needed basis. It's five minutes away from my home, so I can get there quickly, it has reliable Internet, and it's affordably priced. Even better, they have satellite offices across the Des Moines area, so it's unlikely that all of them would be impacted in a future derecho. I planned that if anything happened to my Internet, that I would immediately get in my car and go to the coworking space.

Sure enough, this quarter, my home Internet became unreliable. It went out two or three times per hour, making it impossible to get anything done. I called the Internet company and it turns out that my neighborhood was experiencing an outage that would take several days to fix.

I hopped in my car and went to the coworking space, where I had a desk, reliable Internet, access to conference rooms, and free beer on tap. My employer never knew that I had an Internet issue, and I damn sure wasn't going to tell them.

My service provider fixed the Internet and everything was back to normal in a few days. This kind of outage doesn't happen very often, but it does happen.

This is yet another reason why I advocate for contingency planning. A few minutes of forethought and asking "what if?" saved my butt. During the week my Internet went out, I had to give an important presentation to a senior executive. Thank God I signed up for that coworking space. The meeting went smoothly and no one even knew that I was in a different space because I kept my webcam turned off.

Another great benefit of coworking spaces is that they're similar no matter where you go. To use a US example, it's like going to the Hampton Inn. Whether you're in Iowa, Florida, or Arizona, the Hampton Inn is the Hampton Inn. Same prices, same amenities, same service, same terrible breakfast.

I went to Orlando on a family vacation. I can do my job from anywhere, so instead of using a day off, I found a coworking space two minutes from my hotel. They used the same booking and payment program like the one in my city. I flew into Orlando late Wednesday night, worked all day Thursday, and logged off to enjoy a nice three-day weekend. Anyway, I digress, but I'm a big fan of coworking spaces.

I've been referring to my day job to explain the benefits of coworking, but that's not the point of this chapter. If you're a full-time author, you need a reliable Internet connection too. Imagine your Internet going out for a week when you have a major book publication and marketing campaign planned. Or, imagine that you're speaking at an important event and need a trusty Internet connection. Full-time authorship is also 100 percent work from home. The problems are the same. If you're serious about your writing business, then you need highly dependable Internet too.

I viewed this entire episode as practice for the full-time writing life one day.

BALANCING DATA AND FEELINGS (A RANT)

Recently, I had the unfortunate displeasure of listening to an unbearable webinar. The topic isn't important, but it was related to data science, and it had nothing to do with my job or writing. I attended merely out of curiosity.

The person presenting on the webinar was a jerk. I didn't like them from the moment they opened their mouth because they were unfriendly to the moderators. They said something that, if I could have responded, I would have refuted.

They were talking about the importance of making data-driven decisions. They said, "A person without any data to back up their opinions is just a person with feelings." I wish I could have captured the condescending, arrogant tone in which the person said it. The underlying assumption was that in the business world, people who make decisions with data are better than people who don't, which is total bullshit.

If you've read this series, then you know that I believe in making data-driven decisions whenever possible. Data is extraordinarily important to the writer of the future—I don't need to say that again because I've said it a thousand times. And you've read chapters in this series where I dug deeply into data. But numbers are not the only thing that matters.

I've worked with many "data heads" in my professional and writing life. My experience is that people who make decisions *solely* based on data usually end up making decisions that are just as bad, if not worse, than people who make decisions with no data at all.

The "feelings" that this speaker spoke so poorly about are underrated. It's why in virtually every company in America (and probably the rest of the world), you have leaders at the top who make decisions based on data and analytics, but those decisions often are not what employees would recommend (if employees were ever in a position to counsel their senior leaders, which never happens). Companies sometimes make decisions that are contrary to their customers' interests as well.

Take Google. How many apps and services do they kill that *their customers and employees love,* but they don't serve Google's interests?

Or your local utility. I recently disputed a charge on my Internet bill. They tried to charge *me* for asking for a technician to visit my home and diagnose Internet issues when the outage was *their fault.* I called to complain, and the representative told me that the company had implemented a new service charge, but that they always waived it if customers called to complain. She even told me—on a recorded line—that employees didn't like it because it increased the number of phone calls and angry customers. But a bean counter executive somewhere was probably looking at the number of service calls the company was incurring, and they did some voodoo math that justified charging customers for service calls to recoup costs. I guarantee you that whoever made this decision did not consider the company's reputation. At some point, someone probably said, "This is a terrible idea because it's not fair for customers," and the bean counter probably replied with, "Fair doesn't pay the bills," not understanding the root cause of the increased service calls to begin with. It's always better to fix the root cause than to charge the customer for it, but hey, nobody listens to me.

When every decision you make is about numbers, then your customers become numbers too. No one likes being a number.

I once worked for an insurance company that handled customer complaints and segmented them into different "buckets." Once, I overheard a colleague tell a customer "I'm sorry, ma'am, you got put in the wrong customer bucket." I would have loved to know how that woman felt about being "put" in a bucket.

Feelings *must* be a part of any major decision. If I had to attribute a percentage, I'd say that any decision regarding your writing business (or any business for that matter) should be 80 percent data-driven and 20 percent feelings-driven. It's the feelings that allow you to connect with your audience and serve their interests. The data exists merely to help you determine the best way to do that. But too many people lose sight of that.

I look forward to the day when people will demonstrate a more balanced approach to solving the world's problems.

So, if I had been able to respond to the jerk who said, "A person without data to back up their opinions is just a person with feelings," I would have responded with, "A person with no feelings to back up their data is an asshole."

CREATING A BOOK WALLET

In Volume 1 of this series, I wrote about the idea of a "Book Marketing Plugin" that stores the metadata for your books so you can recall them easily when you are marketing.

I wrote:

———

I envision a browser plugin that gives you easy access to all of your book metadata so that if you need it, you can select the book in the plugin, and the plugin will auto-populate most of the book's info for you. The plugin might also automatically take you to any folders on your computer for that specific book so you don't have to click around to find the right folders.

Think of it like a password wallet like LastPass, LogMeIn, or the Safari keychain, but for your books. Pick the book you want, and the plugin auto-populates as much data as it can. If desired, you could export data from the plugin too. You could also integrate the plugin into a database so that the database feeds the plugin.

Database idea aside, I don't believe this would be too difficult to program.

In 2020, I did a lot of database work when I was creating my automated sales database. Part of that work *was* creating a database with all of my books and their metadata. I abandoned that because the sales database was more important (and more difficult) at the time. Now that I have some more free time, I wanted to revisit this initial database work.

What does a book database need to have to fuel a plugin like the one I described?

It would need:

- Title
- Subtitle
- Author name
- Series name
- Series number
- Names of other contributors
- A low-resolution image of the book cover
- Price in each major currency (for each format)
- Date of publication (for each format)
- BISAC categories
- Keywords
- Book Description
- Unique identifier such as ISBN, ASIN, and other retailer-specific codes
- Print page count
- Print trim size
- Audiobook narrator
- Audiobook length

- File size
- Formats available
- Major retailers that stock the book (with links)
- Number of Reviews
- Review average
- Testimonials

The database would store all of these fields for every book you publish. I call the database a "book wallet," because that's what it really is.

I would also include a few extra fields based on my preferences, such as versioning for my book's interior and book description, as well as fields that capture price changes and when I changed them.

This data can be filtered, pivoted, or manipulated in virtually any way because it's a simple spreadsheet. Each book has a unique ID, and that ID indicates all of the fields above for that book.

I can create a database like this over a weekend. I could also pay someone to compile it for me. Once it's built, it becomes a powerful tool that can help me:

- Feed a marketing plugin like the one I described
- Build an ONIX data feed
- Review the actual metadata for my books compared to what exists in the database (for when I'm doing a "patrol," as I mentioned earlier in this book)

And more.

DEAR AMAZON, APPLE, GOOGLE, AND OTHER BOOK RETAILERS

I'm writing this open letter to you as players who have immense sway in the publishing industry. You have the power to shape the future of the author profession.

Your action (or inaction) will determine the trajectory of publishing as we know it. And you have the power to do some tremendous good, and it won't cost you very much money at all.

My demand is simple: create a book publishing-specific application programming interface (API) for authors to use.

As you know, an API allows a developer to interact with your servers and download data in a manner that you dictate. Controlling the dispensation of your data through APIs is better than allowing developers to "scrape" data from your servers. Web scraping is unethical.

Amazon, you know this better than anyone. How many people have you banned because they scraped data from your website? Data scraping is done to create a competitive advantage, and it can be difficult on your servers.

Amazon, you also know that you offer one of the best APIs in the world: the Amazon Product Advertising API. With clean documentation, easy-to-use instructions, you have set the standard for how APIs are created. Apple and Google, you didn't do a bad job in this area either.

You're probably wondering, "Why is an author asking us for a publishing-specific API?"

Authors need API access because:

- As we become more prolific, it is cumbersome to log in to several different dashboards to upload and manage our books. Being able to interface with an API would make this easier.
- We are finding increasingly sophisticated ways to think about our books. One of those is thinking about our books as data. We need ways to see how our books are performing across all retailers. When I say "performing," I don't mean sales (although that would be nice if you could help us with that too), but metadata. Is my book priced appropriately on Amazon and Apple? Which version of a book description did I upload to all retailers? Did I even upload the right book? These are questions that authors will soon have as more authors become super-prolific. I define "super-prolific" as anything over 50 books. At that point, those authors are practically publishers. If they need to make changes to multiple books, those changes can take hours.

I understand the concerns from your perspective. Do you really want to give API access to authors who, as a class, are not terribly tech-savvy? After all, APIs are not for the faint of heart and the transmission of data cleanly and correctly is important. You need a competent developer to work with APIs; this task should not be left to regular people.

But consider this: you control the standards. You don't have to make the API so that any author can use it. You just need to make it available. Authors who don't understand it will just hire someone who does. And when they do, a new cottage industry will emerge: publishing metadata experts. As you're aware, this already exists in the traditional publishing sector. Publishers use the ONIX standard to publish and manage books on your retail platforms. I even suspect that your biggest book aggregators are using ONIX too. The ONIX standard is written so that authors can use it too if they have the right software. It's so complicated that most authors will run away screaming, but those who need it and can afford it would use the standard. But they can't do that if you don't allow them.

The ONIX standard is not perfect, but it's a suitable alternative for writers of the future.

You may also be thinking, "We already offer APIs." But it's not that easy.

Amazon, your API can only be used to direct traffic to your website and to make sales. It's available in your Amazon Associates Program, and any affiliate who does not make sales through the API can be choked off from access. You don't allow API access for non-sales purposes. You would need to develop a publishing-specific API for authors, or permit authors to use your product advertising API for other purposes, such as monitoring the metadata of their books. Sure, metadata monitoring doesn't make sales per se, but also consider that if an author accidentally lists a book at the wrong price and doesn't realize it for several months, you lose money too. If an author has an accidental typo in a book description, you also lose money. Allowing authors to manage this information at a global level helps to improve the quality of self-published books overall, which is something that I hope you would support.

Apple, I have the same concerns with you as I do with Amazon.

Google, maybe your API is okay to use for metadata management, maybe it's not. You don't offer any official documentation.

If you'd like to take the next steps, here are my recommendations:

- Create a clear publishing API so authors can hire developers to create automated publishing solutions. Or, permit authors to use your existing API for non-sales purposes. Or, allow authors to use the ONIX standard to publish and manage their books.
- Reduce reliance on your dashboards to make changes to books.
- In your existing API documentation, explicitly permit users to gather data for non-competitive purposes, such as monitoring their metadata. You have the power to monitor and restrict access accordingly. I'm not asking you to allow bad actors to use your platforms. I'm merely asking you to allow me to use your API to manage my intellectual property.
- Provide resources to help the new cottage industry of metadata experts to help authors help themselves and reduce the burden on your servers and support staff.

Again, you have the power to change the trajectory of the author profession. Allow API access and you will change the author profession as we know it. Imagine a world where an author can upload a book to your platform with the click of a button, and it's perfectly conditioned and meets your quality and data standards. I dream of a world where books (data) flow easily between authors and retailers, and everyone makes more money as a result of this efficiency.

If you have any questions, call me.

ARTIFICIAL INTELLIGENCE: REQUESTS FOR COMMENT AT ALLI

The Alliance of Independent Authors released a request for comments around artificial intelligence. Depending on when you read this, the comment period is probably over, but I recommend that you read the article and comments anyway, if only to see how little activity there was.

ALLi wanted to know authors' thoughts on artificial intelligence so it can advocate on their behalf. Almost no one responded. Does this mean that authors don't care about AI, or was it just bad timing?

I don't know, but I suspect the former.

When you're an indie author trying to make it, you've got a thousand other things to think about. You're worried about how you're going to pay for editing and cover design. You're worried about whether your work is any good. You're fighting the noble war on book formatting and learning how to produce paperbacks that pass quality assurance. You're worried about the fact that your books aren't selling at the level you want. You're seeing everyone else doing better than you and wonder if you're doing something wrong.

And then there's self-doubt, writer's block, and the

emotional aspect of being a writer. And your family. And your job. And then, if you're lucky, there's business and taxes!

Artificial intelligence just isn't high on the list of most authors right now, and that's understandable.

Consider this multi-part test that might explain why authors aren't interested.

- **Is it relevant to beginners?** New writers need to understand the process of publishing by going through it *at least* once. Otherwise, they won't be interested because, in the early years, the process consumes all of their attention and resources.

- **Does it interfere with the writer's need to be comfortable?** Writers who have published at least a few books move on to the intermediate level, which can last a long time. They need to be *comfortable* by making enough money from their work. I define "enough" as enough to recoup the costs of production plus a little profit. Once the money isn't a worry, writers' awareness expands. If they're making money, they're less preoccupied with craft too, which frees up some of their attention.

- **Is there social proof?** Writers need to feel that a subject they are pursuing "belongs" in the writing life. They might be interested in something conceptually, but it doesn't become real until they see others making money with it and believe they can too.

- **Is it easy to use?** Writers must be able to use a tool or technology easily. Even non-techy writers must be able to use it.

Emerging technology can meet one or more parts of the test, but it won't become mainstream until it meets all the parts.

If you consider the test, then you can see why AI is not taking off for writers yet. So many writers are just worried about finishing their first book, or making enough money to feel comfortable, or understanding how to run a better business.

For a technology to matter, it has to have social proof and ease of use. We aren't there yet. Most AI tools (with a few notable exceptions such as copywriting tools) are *not* easy to use and require programming knowledge. That won't do.

However, this creates an opening for authors who can see opportunity; if they're willing to adopt technology that doesn't meet all elements of the test, they will be early adopters. If they're fortunate and smart about how they use it, they will be rewarded.

That said, it's still unfortunate that ALLi didn't receive much participation. As I'll discuss in the next section, authors' disinterest in AI will probably cause problems for us as a whole in the near future.

AI FOR CONTENT SUMMARIZATION

In Volume 4 of this series, I wrote about an idea called a "Publishing Content Curation Service."

Well, I stumbled across a developer who created something very similar. Before I discuss that, here's what I wrote:

———

Ever since 2010ish, authors have had to navigate a never-ending amount of information on how to be a better author, marketer, and businessperson. There are services such as "The Hot Sheet" by Jane Friedman and The Writer's Knowledge Base by Elizabeth Spann Craig that curate self-publishing knowledge and each of these services is great in their own way. But there is no single service that I know of that can capture everything.

Eight years ago, I would have recommended that someone do this manually, but even a full-time curator would be embarking on a fool's errand. These days, I believe artificial intelligence can solve the problem. An AI can consume blog posts, books, podcasts, YouTube videos, and even comments on social media and contextualize them.

So many news articles these days are written and created by artificial intelligence, so AI already has the capability to consume content and create context. If it can do that, then it can also organize and recommend content based on what you are looking for, and aim to recommend the "right content to the right user at the right time."

Imagine wanting to know the hottest marketing trends. The service could spin a narrative about what people are doing right now based on recent content. It could even spin you a narrative based on how a certain marketing technique has evolved, such as Amazon Ads. As such, it might be able to warn you about certain practices that are either out of favor or no longer effective.

⸻

I also went further and discussed how technology like this can help with the discoverability problem, but I won't go into that here.

I was searching for a developer to help me with an unrelated project, and I encountered one who had a project on his resume that caught my eye.

It was a "Financial News Summarizer," which, in his words, was "a system that intakes financial news articles and simplifies the article into a quick and easy-to-read summary. This program uses NLTK, BeautifulSoup, and Flask."

On Github, the documentation reads as follows:

"FINS (Financial News Summarizer) uses a combination of web scraping, extractive summarization and Flask-RESTful to create a simple API that summarizes financial news articles. Extractive summarization works by assigning weights to the sentences through a series of tokenization. This program is built to create summaries by only using sentences with a weighted score above three standard deviations from the mean weight, capturing only the most important content."

Wow. Tech jargon aside, this is fascinating. Imagine receiving an email update weekly with a summary of major events in the self-publishing space:

- Who did your favorite podcast interviewers talk to this week, and what tips did they offer?
- What's happening at the Alliance of Independent Authors' blog?
- Are there any industry statistics you need to be aware of that are in the news?

You can certainly look up the developer's tool, as he was a nice guy and more people should know about the work he did in this space. I share it merely to prove my earlier point that this technology already exists, and it's available for us to use. It's just not easy yet. Someone can make it easier.

MORE AI SUMMARIZATION EXPERIMENTS

In the last chapter, I discussed AI content summarization and how a developer I networked with created a tool that created financial summaries.

I couldn't help myself in researching other tools that could do this, just to see how good they are.

I took the previous chapter and ran it through two free AI tools to see how well they summarized the main points of the chapter. Does the technology produce usable summaries?

One tool was called Sassbook. Here's the summary it provided me:

An AI can consume blog posts, books, podcasts, YouTube videos, and even comments on social media and contextualize them. The service could spin a narrative about what people are doing right now based on recent content. It could even spin you a narrative based on how a certain marketing technique has evolved, such as Amazon Ads. As such, it might be able to warn you about certain practices that are either out of favor or no longer effective. It can also organize and recommend content based on what you are looking for, and aim to recommend the "right content to the right user at the right time."

Nope. It just took the sentences that it thought were the most important.

I also ran the chapter through TLDR, another tool. Here's how it did:

In Volume 4 of this series, I wrote about an idea called "Publishing Content Curation Service."

Well, I stumbled across a developer who created something very similar.

So many news articles these days are written and created by artificial intelligence, so AI already has the capability to consume content and create context.

This program is built to create summaries by only using sentences with a weighted score above three standard deviations from the mean weight, capturing only the most important content."

Imagine receiving an email update weekly with a summary of major events in the self-publishing space?

I share it merely to prove my earlier point that this technology already exists, and it's available for us to use.

Even bigger nope.

Hmm...perhaps the technology is not as advanced as I thought. Or, premium programs are doing a better job. I'm not willing to pay to experiment.

Does that mean this technology will never work? No, but it's not where it needs to be yet. Give it a few years and it will be dangerous.

AI CHARACTER GENERATOR

I stumbled upon LitRPG Adventures, which is a service by LitRPG author and developer Paul Bellow that provides AI-generated characters, stories, and worlds to use in their tabletop gaming and LitRPG stories.

Paul's service isn't the only one. There are other apps such as Sudowrite that provide a similar service.

Paul writes the following on the website: "Save time and money with our AI D&D generators and library. Members of our growing community get instant access to our fantasy RPG generators powered by GPT-3 from OpenAI. Members also get access to our growing RPG library full of all sorts of tabletop RPG content."

Tabletop gaming and LitRPG are all about character data and statistics. In the RPG world, characters have "strength," "defense," and other characteristics that determine how well they will do in battle.

To relate this to authors, you can use Paul's content as fodder for your novel. If you need a character, use one from his library. The character comes with a backstory, a profession, a race, and other elements that make them fully fleshed out and ready to import into your story.

Licensing issues aside (which Paul addresses in the terms of service), this is an interesting concept. I heard an interview with author Yudhanjaya Wijeratne on "The Creative Penn Podcast," where he talked about using artificial intelligence as a co-writer. He used software to help him write scientific elements in his bestselling book *The Salvage Crew*. It seems that this method, while still among early adopters, will soon seep into the mainstream.

I also see immense value in a tool like this when writing short stories. Sometimes, I like to write about random people. A character generator could help with that.

Three years from now, more people will be doing it, especially if more services like Paul's make it easier for authors to benefit from AI without having to be a programmer.

BECOME THE WRITER OF
THE FUTURE

THE FUTURE OF KDP: THOUGHT
EXERCISE

As I write this, there is chatter in the United States about Congress (finally) passing bills that will limit the power of big tech companies like Amazon, Google, and Facebook.

The US barely has a functioning government right now. Both political parties never agree on anything, so it's odd to see them agree on something now.

Reasons this is a hot topic right now include:

- Facebook lost trust after the Cambridge Analytica scandal in the 2016 election, which almost certainly contributed to Donald Trump winning the election to become a Republican president. I suspect that Democratic Party wanted revenge.
- Tech companies have faced growing criticisms for antitrust practices. Examples include Facebook buying WhatsApp and Instagram.
- Social media platforms and YouTube have faced criticism for silencing far left and far right political voices for various reasons, some legitimate, some not

so legitimate. This reached a crescendo during the pandemic and the 2020 election cycle.

- Social media platforms en masse permanently banned Donald Trump after the riots at the US Capitol on January 6, 2021. Now Republicans wanted revenge.
- Congress held a series of testimonies with big tech giant CEOs. In one of these sessions, Jeff Bezos, then-CEO of Amazon, admitted that the company had potentially used third-party seller data to create new private label products to compete in the marketplace, among other serious antitrust violations. Also, during these testimonies, Congress revealed how woefully out-of-touch they were with the advancement in technology. (Is it in any surprise with the average Congressional age being 59 to 62 years old? Our representatives frequently die in office, and since they get such great healthcare, they live a long time.) Anyway, Congress didn't want to look stupid again, so they did their homework.
- Amazon keeps making the headlines for all the wrong reasons; its suppression of workers' right to unionize in Bessemer, Alabama, stories of drivers having no time to take bathroom breaks, and more.

Now, here we are. Tech companies have pissed off both political parties in the United States, and they have lost trust with American citizens (and the rest of the world). At the time of this writing, they're staring at six potential antitrust bills that will change their industry as we know it. The United States isn't the first to take action against them. Other countries have been attempting to curb big their power too.

Here's how that could affect self-published authors.

One of the bills is called the American Online Innovation Act, and it attempts to regulate and/or break up tech companies, including Amazon.

In reviewing the House of Representatives' first draft of the bill, it reads (with enumeration and formatting removed for readability), "It shall be unlawful for a person operating a covered platform...to engage in any conduct...that advantages the covered platform operator's own products...over those of another business user; excludes or disadvantages the products... relative to the covered platform operator's own products...or discriminates among similarly situated business users."

In short, this is saying that companies like Amazon can't disadvantage third-party sellers by prioritizing its own products in search. This could also be interpreted to apply to books too. Amazon won't be able to promote Amazon Publishing titles as rampantly as it does now. Kristine Kathryn Rusch points out that this could apply to Kindle Unlimited titles too. If that's true, then all of the marketing advantages of KDP Select will disappear overnight.

Kristine Kathryn Rush also quotes Michael Cader of Publishers Lunch and offers some additional insights.

"For Amazon," Cader writes, "that would likely mean divesting most arms of their publishing octopus, including much if not all of Audible, plus Brilliance, Amazon Publishing, Kindle Direct Publishing, and probably CreateSpace. It might apply to divesting AbeBooks as well.

"Sit with that for a moment. Amazon might have to get rid of everything that makes their indie publishing arm possible. Amazon could do a few things with it. They might sell the pieces. If those arms aren't making a lot of money (in corporate terms), they might simply shut them down."

What would happen if Amazon divested itself of Kindle Direct Publishing?

The best-case scenario would be if they spun their publishing arm into a separate company. It might operate with increased regulation, but we'd still be able to self-publish.

The worst-case scenario would be if Amazon shut it down. The Kindle reading division would probably continue, but (self) publishing on it would not. Self-published authors would lose a giant chunk of revenue. Authors exclusive to Amazon would lose everything. Everything. More likely than not, traditional publishers would be able to continue publishing on Amazon. My understanding is that the Kindle Direct Publishing division does not oversee traditional publishers.

The doomsday scenario would be if Amazon sold KDP. Who would they sell it to?

Consider if Penguin Random House (PRH) bought it. Overnight, you'd be at the mercy of a traditional publisher who would now have a near-monopoly on the self-published market. Don't forget that PRH also owns Author Solutions, a notorious vanity publishing company. Might we be folded into Author Solutions and be forced to pay to continue publishing on the platform, for a reduced royalty and tougher publishing rules? That's really, really scary.

And if you're thinking "But that would be a monopoly, right?", consider that Congress is only focused on big tech. For all other industries, Congress (and our Supreme Court) has done very little to curb antitrust operations. In Iowa, our Internet is run by a duopoly. If you don't like one, you have to go to the other, and they both engage in the same bullshit tactics. I don't see the federal or state governments doing anything about *that*. I digress.

But, no matter what happens, I predict that if traditional publishers are smart and learned *anything* from the ebook revolution, they'll seize on the opportunity. If they get around to embracing AI and data, then they'll have tremendous advantages that I've been warning about for the last few years. The current boom cycle indies are experiencing will be over, and authors will believe that they have no other way to make money but to sign horrible contracts again.

Everything is cyclical. Traditional publishing is out now, but it won't always be. It'll be back, just in a different form. It's just a matter of time, and the breakup of Amazon and the divestment of KDP Publishing could facilitate it.

Do I want Amazon to be broken up? I don't know. I would hope that they can comply with regulations and play fairly. I would also hope that if Congress does something for a change, that they will do it right and empower government agencies to regulate. But I recognize that that has consequences for my author career, my livelihood, and my future as an author.

The good news? If you're not reliant on Amazon for all your income, then you'll be less impacted by such a change. That's why it pays to start building an audience on other platforms now so that you aren't forced to later.

Such an event would be a mass extinction event for indie authors. The authors who survive will do so because they had a sound long-term strategy.

Will any of this happen? I don't know. Despite Congress's rare bipartisan agreement, I'll believe the bills when they're passed and enforced. Too many things can happen. The bills could get watered down. A major political event could force Congress to pay attention to something else, and this moment will fade away. Or, Congress didn't really want to implement these bills, and they were just sending a warning shot to big tech companies and it could be several more years until we see true antitrust legislation.

In any case, it pays to think ahead and be prepared if the scenario comes to pass.

GOOGLE'S AI NARRATION INITIATIVE

I learned that Google has started a beta for artificial intelligence narration for audiobooks. I've written at length in previous volumes about my thoughts on AI narration, so I won't rehash them here, but I am intrigued.

Google now sells public domain titles on the Play Store with AI narration, which, as far as I know, is the first time this has been done outside of China. As with all betas that Google does, one has to watch with bated breath and a healthy dose of skepticism.

That said, I downloaded a few public domain titles and listened to them. The narration wasn't good, but it wasn't bad either. It clearly sounded like an AI was reading the book, but it sounded a hell of a lot better than current voice-to-text software on phones and computers. The voice still reads too fast and doesn't handle sentence breaks or proper nouns well. Still, it's promising.

With any new technology, people are quick to judge or write it off without understanding the rate at which technology advances. I'd give Google's effort a C-. In five years, however, if they continue the program and continue improving the technology, it'll be a B+ or an A-, enough for customers to start paying attention. Then, overnight, the technology will be mainstream and everyone will be using it.

Of course, it's hard to know how this specific technology will work, but that's usually the story.

Being able to publish your books on Google Play and then check a box that makes AI narration available along with your ebook edition will be a winning proposition. You could get your book into audio without any extra effort on your part. Then, you could also create a traditional audiobook with a narrator. It's not an "either/or." It's an "and."

The watershed moment will occur when AI narration is almost indistinguishable from an amateur narrator. If the AI edition is cheaper than a traditional audiobook, customers will split into three groups.

The first group will *never* listen to AI audiobooks, much like some readers today who will never read ebooks and prefer print.

The second group will *only* buy AI audio, forgoing traditional narration in favor of cheaper prices and convenience. These readers probably listen to audiobooks only for information, or they listen at two- or three-times' speed, so the performance of a narrator isn't as important to them.

The third group will prefer traditional narration for the authors and narrators they love but will buy AI audio for authors they're less sure about. AI audio will become a way to test an author's work, and if it's good, they'll buy future books in traditional audio format.

That's an interesting future. Will Google shape it? I doubt it, but we'll see.

WHY I LOVE COPYRIGHT LICENSING

I recently licensed an article that I wrote for money. Cool! I signed a contract, wrote the article to spec, and got paid.

Here's why I love copyright: there was a clause in the contract that said, "If we reprint the article, we'll pay you again."

One morning, I woke up to an email from the company saying that they liked the article so much that they were going to reprint it in a book, and that they would be depositing a tidy sum into my bank account. It was on a Monday morning too, which made it a great start to my week.

Ka-ching!

That's the beauty of copyright. It will keep making you money for your entire life plus 70 years, and if you're smart about the contracts you sign and the people you do business with, you'll wake up to unexpected but pleasant paydays.

CONVERSATION WITH AN ASPIRING
AUTHOR

I spoke with an aspiring author by telephone early this quarter. This person wanted to publish their first book but was paralyzed and overwhelmed by the sheer amount of information out there. They didn't know whether to use a traditional publisher or self-publish, but they leaned toward a publisher because (insert every publishing myth you can think of).

"A publisher taking a chance on me will want me to succeed."

"Having a publisher behind me makes me more legitimate."

"A publisher will get my book into bookstores."

"A publisher will take care of everything so I can just write."

This was just in the first five minutes of our conversation.

I talk to authors all the time, and I've learned that some people are going to do what they're going to do even if it hurts them and you try to warn them. Therefore, I don't give advice. I just give people information and they can do whatever they want with it. I try to give people a realistic expectation of what the writing life is actually like, not what they want it to be. New authors are too hard-headed to listen to common sense sometimes. I say that out of love and respect because I was hard-headed at the beginning of my writing journey too.

I discussed the pros and cons of traditional and self-publishing with this author. Their biggest objection to self-publishing was that they had low self-esteem. I explained that feelings of low self-esteem are prevalent in the community and that it was okay. That freaked the author out. Then I tried to dispel some of the myths around traditional publishing, then I discussed the downsides of self-publishing. I tried as much as possible to paint an accurate picture for this author. That's what they needed, not advice.

I have no idea which path the author will choose, but that's ultimately their decision. However, it got me thinking about how I desperately need a book in my catalogue that I can point beginners to. My book *The Indie Author Atlas* sort of does this by creating a curriculum of things to learn, but not quite.

The conversation was helpful for me because it kept me grounded with the issues that aspiring authors continue to face. It's important for me to stay connected with those so that my books remain helpful to people, even though I'm much further down the road.

ENTERPRISE SELF-PUBLISHING

Mike Shatzkin published a blog article about what he feels will be the next wave of self-publishing: self-publishing enterprises. You can find it by searching his blog for "enterprise self-publishing."

Shatzkin is a traditional publishing industry veteran who sometimes gets flak from the indie community, but he offers valuable (if sometimes a little too romantic) insights into the history of traditional publishing.

His thoughts on enterprise self-publishing were half "he's onto something" and half "he's a little late to the party."

He writes, *"What I believe we are on the verge of seeing is that waves of entities will discover that they can clearly benefit from publishing books. Think of this as enterprise self-publishing. Every law firm, accounting firm, consulting firm, retailer, political campaign, cause organization, charity, and church, synagogue, or mosque is only a bit of imagination and effort away from books that can promote any variety of missions. These will be books delivered by a vast unaffiliated network of entities doing publishing as a "function", not publishing as a "business."*

Shatzkin foresees a second tsunami of books on the market,

this time by corporations who realize they can create a book with value for cheaper than they can pay a marketing campaign. Shatzkin isn't the first to express this sentiment; I've heard others talk about this as well.

On the one hand, I agree with him. He envisions an industry where books are published by *businesses*. He uses the examples of small businesses, but that's where he gets it wrong. Small business owners are already doing this, using books as calling cards for their businesses. This is especially prevalent on YouTube. Sean Cannell and Benji Travis of Think Media (a YouTube channel and digital media company) published a best-selling book about YouTube strategies. While they are savvy influencers, publishing isn't their main goal; but their book made them a lot of money and helped them serve their audience, which was already over one million when they published. YouTube, LinkedIn, and other social media sites are full of stories like Sean and Benji's, with entrepreneurs, executives, and small business owners sharing books about their personal experiences.

I believe it's more likely to see big enterprises entering publishing. KFC experimented with this in 2017 during a Mother's Day marketing campaign by writing a steamy romance novel called *Tender Wings of Desire* starring Colonel Sanders. The book cover showed a muscular Colonel Sanders atop a stormy moor with a swooning woman and—wait for it—a bucket of chicken. Despite how cheesy it sounds, the book was *surprisingly* well-written and garnered great reviews and marketing buzz.

KFC released the book around Mother's Day because that's one of its biggest sales days. The company actively targets moms in its marketing.

It's not hard to see companies like KFC hiring a skilled ghostwriter (like they did with *Tender Wings of Desire*) and publishing a romance series that is written to market. Taken a step further, this would become, as Shatzkin correctly pointed out, a function of KFC's marketing department. They'll do it until it stops working.

Or, imagine Taco Bell (owned by Yum! Brands, the same company that owns KFC) publishing a military science fiction series to reach a male demographic.

Companies may try this because it's a different type of revenue stream. Invest $1,000 in the creation of a book and it becomes an asset that generates income every month. They never have to unpublish it. That's appealing, but only if it works. In the case of KFC, the books will need to get people into their restaurants.

The pandemic has businesses looking for ways to rebalance their portfolios. One sector where this is happening is in real estate, with private equity buying up housing stock since the stock market is so volatile.

Companies also may not try this because there isn't a huge return and there are other ways they can make more money faster.

But Shatzkin's sentiment is accurate. I do believe it could happen, but not for a long time. Eventually, businesses will find something else to chase.

If it does happen, though, a smart indie could position themselves to major brands as an enterprise novelist or nonfiction writer. All it takes is for one or two brands to hire you for your writing and publishing expertise, and you'll be paid handsomely in what may ultimately be a small window of opportunity. If I'm wrong, it could become a nice freelancing avenue.

HITTING BESTSELLER LISTS

Benjamin Franklin said that two things are certain in life: death and taxes. I'd like to add a third to the list: indie authors trying to find a way to hit a bestseller list, even just for a day so they can have the coveted " Bestseller" or "USA Today Bestseller" behind their name. Every few years, this comes back in full force, and droves of authors, as if mind-controlled, start clambering for the titles.

I remember early in my career when authors would use box set schemes to hit bestseller lists. One author in particular offered a buy-in program where authors could pay to get into box sets that were guaranteed to hit lists. Not only did venues learn about it and try to police the behavior, but many of those authors also got their accounts terminated at retailers because the actions required to hit the list bordered on unethical and violated terms of service. And still, authors want that title behind their name more than anything. You can't reason with them.

The *New York Times* has made it more difficult to land on their bestseller lists, primarily because of scammy indie authors. I'm surprised other bestseller lists haven't done the same.

If I was an author with six-figure sales who, all math considered, could easily hit a list with a little help, would I consider it? Sure, but only because I would be so close anyway, and only because I'd have the fan base to do it.

But the people who most often want to do this do not have stellar book sales, and they think that having an illustrious title behind their name will help that.

I've seen studies over the years that have shown that authors with a major newspaper behind their names tend to sell more books. Maybe that's true. But I believe in authenticity and integrity above sales. If your name even has the distant smell of impropriety, that's not worth it in my opinion. I'd rather readers buy my books based on their inherent value, not because I gamed the system. If that means I never achieve a fancy title, so be it. Writing has never been about titles to me.

I always shake my head every time I see these schemes pop up again.

AUTHORS ARE TIRED OF AI

I talked to a few influencers who expressed concern that discussing artificial intelligence was hurting their audience engagement. Because artificial intelligence doesn't help writers write books faster or sell more books, they just aren't interested in it.

I predicted this from the beginning. I've said many times on my channels that authors won't be interested in this technology until it can provide something concrete and tangible for them. In other words, "What's in it for me?"

However, that's not how artificial intelligence works. If you talk to any data scientist who specializes in this technology, they will most likely tell you that artificial intelligence is about incremental progress. It is not about short-term profit. But so many companies and people approach it wanting immediate profit from it when the real profit is long-term.

How can we discuss the emerging technology in a way that will be engaging to writers so that they can see the vision of the type of world they can create with it?

I see this vision clearly: authors can use artificial intelligence to become near "cyborgs," using technology to assist them in accomplishing every task of the writing and publishing process faster and more accurately. They can also use tools to own their data and make more targeted decisions that will make them money, improve the quality of their books, improve readers' enjoyment of their books, and even improve the quality of their lives because AI will permeate every aspect of our society.

Alternatively, how can we communicate the dangers of this technology so that we can proactively seek to prevent its dystopian aspects that are sure to come about if we do nothing?

I also see this clearly: a society of haves and have-nots where authors and publishers with the most money can afford to take advantage of sophisticated technology, and authors who failed to embrace the technology will be deprived of opportunities and therefore quit or make less money. Just as I mentioned previously, AI will permeate every area of our lives, and not being able to succeed in the writing space will make these writers miserable. They will be left behind, forgotten, and mocked for not embracing the technology earlier. Traditional publishers will figure out the technology too, and they'll be so good at it that authors will have no choice but to sign their contracts again if they want to sell books.

I don't mean to be alarmist, but I do believe that if we do not put ourselves in the driver's seat to shape the kind of future we want, others (read: corporations) will shape the future for us. We won't like what we see.

But people still aren't interested in this technology, even if I use sharp imagery. Why?

It doesn't make authors' production processes smoother yet. It doesn't help writers write books. It doesn't help with marketing right now outside of copywriting. It doesn't offer any other efficiencies.

In short, it's merely entertaining to watch and muse about, but it doesn't yet bring about any real change for an author who is just concerned about writing their book and marketing it. Watching amusing doesn't pay the bills and it doesn't build platforms. So what are we to do?

I don't know, but I don't believe it's fair to blame authors for not being interested. Sure, they should be, and sure, we would be in a better place as a profession if we did, but it's human nature not to care about something until it affects you.

I wish I knew the answer. If I did, I would offer some solutions and a roadmap. But I fear that if the apathy continues, we will either see stunting of growth of artificial intelligence in the author space or we're not going to like what's coming.

I don't have any solutions for the community at large other than for influencers to keep talking about it. But I do have some advice for YOU.

Every author can take steps to understand this technology, its promise, and how they can weave it into their platform.

I suggest that it is up to you to figure out your artificial intelligence strategy. At this point, no one is going to do it for you, and I don't see anyone dedicating themselves to creating advanced tools to help authors as a whole. If they do, they'll do it without too much input from the authors who need it most—those who will be left behind.

That means that it's all up to you. Your choices will be limited. But if you keep following the technology and keep your eyes open to opportunities, you will find benefits, and you will gain long-term advantages.

In this series alone, I have discussed many tools that you can be on the lookout for in the future to become the writer of the future.

The future arrives daily. The future of artificial intelligence for your writing career is unfortunately up to you and you alone. Some may see that as a burden, but I see it as an amazing responsibility to explore a future that will look drastically different from today. You can win in that future if you become a student of the technology. That learning begins today.

PUBLISHER CO-OPS?

It's not a proper volume of *Indie Author Confidential* without mentioning a co-op of some kind!

I was watching a series of interviews with Marxist economist Richard Wolff, and he was explaining a concept he believes in called "Democracy at Work."

I don't ascribe to either United States political party because I believe they're both terrible. I consider myself a populist and anti-establishment. I agree with many liberal progressive policies, but I agree with some conservative ones as well.

I believe the United States is in a transition period because capitalism isn't working. What we're transitioning to, I have no idea, and that's what makes the current times we're living in scary.

But anyway, I digress. I like hearing people's ideas because the exchange of ideas, whether you agree with them or not, makes our society better.

Professor Wolff's "Democracy at Work" idea is fascinating. It's a type of socialism, but without the baggage of socialism.

It's not Scandinavian socialism, which many Europeans are familiar with in some form.

It's not Communism, which many countries in the world have unfortunate experiences in.

Instead, it's a reform of capitalism that allows it to remain intact, but with some major changes.

Today in any corporation, the CEO, senior executives, and the board of directors make the major decisions. Orders flow downward. Entry-level associates have no say in how the company is run. If you're an employee and you don't like the direction the company is moving in, you have to find another job. If you're an investor in that company and you don't like what they're doing, you have to sell your shares. You have no power.

The principle behind "Democracy at Work" is to create a cooperative sector where companies are co-ops. In a co-op, employees decide how the business is run, not executives. Employees decide about the products, suppliers, customers, marketing, and more. They decide how decisions get made too.

There are cooperatives in the United States currently, but they are not a popular way to run a business.

I'm sure that you've worked for a company in which you vehemently disagreed with a decision your boss or senior leaders made while wondering at the same time what it would be like if managers listened to their employees. If you worked in a co-op and you were able to convince your colleagues that a decision was wrong, you might be able to stop the company from doing it. You can't do that in today's capitalistic society.

Professor Wolff's vision is a market where the capitalist sector that we have today competes with a cooperative sector. Let's see what happens. Maybe the capitalist companies will do better in a certain industry. Maybe co-ops will do better in others. Maybe co-ops will offer better benefits such as more time off or other benefits that allow people to spend more time with their families. But either way, they will compete against each other. By empowering employees to change the workplaces in which they live, they have the power to improve their lives. After all, they spend more time with their coworkers than they do with their families. Shouldn't it be an enjoyable experience?

We have democracy in our civic lives, so why not in the workplace?

Professor Wolff's strategy isn't perfect. No economic strategy is. And I'm sure there are trade-offs that haven't been considered. But as someone who wants to see our society rebuild crumbling infrastructure and create better opportunities for prosperity for everyone and not just the upper classes, I believe it's a better strategy than doing nothing or continuing the same tactics from the past seventy years.

This got me thinking about what the publishing industry would look like with a cooperative sector.

On one hand, you'd have the Big Five publishers and small presses as we know them today, and on the other hand, you'd have something interesting.

Let's pretend that there exists a publisher called Walrus (Walrus...competing with Penguin. Get it?). Walrus is a publishing co-op run by its employees. Instead of an acquiring editor, the employees of Walrus determine which books to publish. The employees decide which authors to bring on board, the company's general contract terms, and its marketing strategy for its books. They decide who gets marketing dollars too.

What types of decisions might they make? Would they end up aligning with traditional publishers? Maybe.

They might also decide that they don't want to create a portfolio of long-term assets. They only want portfolios of authors' books that sell. If an author doesn't sell and the company can't find a way to fix it, they give the rights back as soon as possible.

A publishing co-op might also have a better idea of what readers in certain segments want because, as a smaller company, they can keep in better touch with booksellers and reader habits.

They might also be better stewards of the Internet and emerging technology.

They might also give their authors some voting rights in how the business is run. That would be interesting...when an author signs with Walrus, they're incentivized to treat the business like they own it. That might lead to some interesting twists on how publishing businesses are run. It might also lead to disaster, but nobody knows.

Co-ops might also give their *readers* a say in how the business is run. Hmm...imagine being a voracious reader in a certain genre and being able to buy shares in Walrus. You, the reader, get a say in the type of books that get published...so you can read them.

You might think, "This could be a bureaucratic nightmare," but remember that employees decide how the company is run and how decisions are made. They would decide if authors and readers can vote, and what those voting rules would be. When we think of bureaucracy, we think of it in terms of hierarchy. This is because everything that goes on in an organization must be approved by leadership. People in the "middle" of a company have their agendas for making sure some things don't get done. I've worked in corporations for a long time—trust me, I would know.

Employees would be incentivized to make their business as efficient as possible. Some of that might involve doing business as usual per capitalistic companies. But the fact that they *don't* have to do the same old tiring, disengaging things is infinitely intriguing and worth exploring in my opinion.

Another thing worth considering is that you can make an argument that a business in the hands of its employees could be more ethical. They might not sacrifice human capital for short-term profit, especially if the collateral is in the very communities they live in. A co-op that runs a manufacturing plant would be less likely to pollute the drinking water in their town, for example.

It's an idea worth exploring, at least in the publishing sector.

A SAD MEMORY

When I was writing an earlier chapter on my marketing strategy, I remembered something sad.

Sometime between 2016 and 2017, I saw a Facebook ad in my newsfeed for a company that wanted to buy the rights to self-published books. I'm paraphrasing the copy on their website, but it read something like, "Are you tired of publishing books that don't sell? Maybe you've spent thousands of dollars of savings and retirement on a dream that never came true. We'd like to buy your books and help you replace those expenses. Select how many books you have in the drop-down below and get a quote. We'll take the books and breathe new life into them, and you can rest assured they are safe with us."

I'm not kidding. A wave of sadness rushed through me as I read it, and I felt it again when I was writing about how authors who write their passion are more likely to burn out when their career doesn't happen.

The company paid absurdly low amounts for books too. If I remember correctly, they paid around $100 per book. Sell the copyright to the hard work you created for $100 so you can pay your bills...

I think about how some authors were probably stupid enough to fall for it. They might have spent thousands of dollars on a career that brought out their self-doubt, alienated them from their spouse, or caused money issues. They might have just had a fight with their spouse about money the night before, then saw this website and decided to sell their books.

The worst part is that the company paid a fraction of what the books were worth. Even the most poorly edited, typo-ridden book is worth more than $100. For the cost of an editor, a new cover, and better positioning, the book might be able to sell better. But authors can't see past the current moment, unfortunately. That book could be worth tens of thousands if not millions. Sure, maybe not, but no book I know of is worth just $100. A book is the output of the human mind, and that's worth a lot of money.

It always comes down to self-esteem and self-doubt. Writers who can't suppress self-doubt always lose. Moreover, writers as a class suffer from self-doubt. It's an occupational hazard.

The people at this company knew this, and they used it to exploit authors. I have less respect for them than I do for scammy marketers. I like to see my scammers coming. These types cloak themselves in authors' emotions and make it seem as if the author is making a choice that will empower them, when all the author will do is regret the decision down the road. Regular scammers just want your money. These people want your soul, and your book is the clearest expression of it.

I hope that this company is no longer around and that their business failed. I also hope there is a special place in hell for them where their punishment is refreshing their sales dashboard every second and seeing that all the work they stole isn't there because the rights were reverted to the authors.

SOME THOUGHTS ON DEATH

"We're all just passing through."

Al Jarreau, one of my favorite jazz and R&B singers, said this while giving a eulogy for George Duke, another jazz legend. That wisdom always stuck with me.

A few years ago, I was a manager. I had a team of 13 great people, a group of peers with whom I got along very well, and I genuinely enjoyed the work. Yet I was unhappy.

I became a manager before I was ready. I thought I knew what I was signing up for, but I didn't. The only reason I did it was because my director at the time believed in me and thought it would be a good growth opportunity. He was right, but probably not in the way he expected. Shortly after hiring me, he left the department, and things were never the same afterward.

I didn't succeed as a manager. Not from a business perspective. I'm not a manager—I'm a leader. I don't find any joy in managing people or situations. I prefer to develop people and help the business meet its goals.

The experience taught me a lot about myself and what I am (and am not) capable of. The truth was that the role was a bad fit for me. When I learned *why* and gazed upon my soul, I discovered that I was capable of being a leader, but not in that environment. That said, I was grateful for the experience because of what it taught me.

The department had a tradition of slow-clapping out people who leave. I got a slow-clap as I carried my box to the elevator that would take me to my new department on the top floor of the building. I appreciated that, and it was bittersweet to leave colleagues I liked.

I entered the elevator, and as it carried me to a new job and new future, I had a strange feeling of cosmic self-awareness, when you connect to the universe for a split second. I was alone —intensely alone despite *just* having been enveloped in respect and love. And waiting, watching the numbers above the elevator doors shift and beep. A brief shiver ran through my body.

I realized that a phase in my life was ending and I was preparing for another. I was standing in that elevator with my box, waiting for the next phase of my life.

Then the doors opened and ended the brief moment of cosmic awareness, and I walked into what was a very fruitful transitional period in my life. During that period, I sought therapy, entered a period of deep self-reflection, and I grew my writing endeavors exponentially. I also became a better father, husband, and son. When COVID-19 hit, I was centered and more equipped to deal with it than most. As I reflect on that moment, only now can I fully appreciate those thirty seconds in the elevator for what they were.

That waiting period in the elevator...maybe that's what death is like.

Life is just a department. You're put on this Earth to do *something*. Whether you're aware of your purpose or not, you accomplish it. When you're done, you get slow-clapped to an elevator that carries you to the great beyond.

We're all just passing through.

While you're here in this "department," how will you spend your time before the claps start?

No one knows when they're going to die. Some people are fortunate enough to live a long life and see it coming, like my 93-year-old grandfather. He spent his final days in hospice. Hospice is one of those rare moments in life as well where you can see someone preparing to leave this world. It's terrifying at the time, but once it's over, you can see the moment for what it truly was.

Others don't see death coming, like the uncle I lost in the Vietnam War who stepped on a landmine and lost his life in an instant.

I don't know whether it's better to see death coming or to die instantly, but I do know that however it happens, I want to make a difference with my time here before the worms get my body.

For me, I can make a difference in several ways:

- Be a good father.
- Be a good husband, brother, and relative.
- Do what I can to make a positive impact in the companies where I work. For me, positive impact doesn't mean profit necessarily. It means making connections with colleagues and making their lives easier.
- Be a good citizen of my community and my country.
- Write novels that educate and entertain people.
- Write books and create content that makes a difference in writers' lives and pushes the profession forward.
- Put good vibes into the universe.

Are those things my purpose? I don't know. I don't think anyone truly knows their purpose. You can choose something that you believe your purpose is and put your energy into it, but that doesn't mean you will have been right. Maybe the purpose we think we are serving isn't the actual purpose. Humans want "big purposes" like changing the world, but maybe our true purposes are micro. Something as subtle as smiling at someone down on their luck or taking the time to help your cousin with a high school project that will ultimately lead to an amazing passion—that could be what we're meant to do. Instead of a big purpose, our purpose might simply be to *be here* on this planet and transmit a certain frequency of attitude that impacts and influences others. That frequency is our personality. Whatever we choose to do within the confines of that frequency (and it has a very wide range) is up to us, but our waves transmit every-where we go, and others' waves wash over us.

Dr. Cornel West says the kingdom of heaven is within us and we should leave a little piece of heaven everywhere we go. I've always agreed with that.

Books are a wonderful way to transmit our frequencies. They are little pieces of heaven and time capsules that offer a look into the times in which we live.

Books are a celebration of life. Every book is a monument to the author. They too can emulate the elevator. Some books transport you to a different realm of thinking, like *The Conquest of Happiness* by Bertrand Russell did for me.

I am confident that when I leave this world, I will be leaving behind a lot of beacons that will continue to transmit long after I'm gone. Not many professions can say that.

I know what I want to do before my time is up, and I do my best to live with passion and purpose every day.

How are you living your passion and purpose for the time you're just passing through?

SIGNPOSTS ALONG THE ROAD

Dean Wesley Smith wrote a wonderful blog post about a concept he called "signposts along the road."

At the time, he was preparing to move out of a condo in downtown Las Vegas to a bigger high-rise penthouse with better views, and he stopped to reflect just how far he'd come in his life as a writer. I'll let you read the article because I thought the way he wrote about it was very touching.

We often don't stop to think about our progress. We're so busy thinking about what's next, how to sell our books, and how to make more money. But there are times when life asks us to stop and reflect on where we are and how we got there. It's our choice whether we listen or not.

Another thing Dean said that I appreciated was that he focused on looking for signs on where he was in his career in his first two decades. Now he doesn't care, but the exercise is amusing to him.

I despise giving out ugly links, but I'll break my rule. You can read his post at

www.deanwesleysmith.com/a-signpost-along-the-road/.

The post got me thinking about the signposts in my life.

The first signpost for me was vivid. It was 2014, and my wife was pregnant with my daughter. We were living in a tiny studio apartment, and my "writing space" was our living room couch. One night, I had gotten my manuscript back from my editor for my second novel, *Theo and the Festival of Shadows*. I stayed up late into the night working on my editor's edits and formatting the ebook version. I remember a great feeling of joy spreading through my body, and I remember saying to myself what a special time this was. Sitting on my couch, working on a second book—how many writers ever got that far? I loved my protagonist, a steadfast and prickly teddy bear with a sword and shield who fights tirelessly to save his owner from a nightmare dimension (think "Toy Story" meets "David Bowie's Labyrinth"). I loved the *process* of writing and publishing a book, even though there was a lot to learn. I think about that moment from time to time because there was something special about it; thinking about it now, it was a signpost.

The next signpost was in 2016 when I was writing *Old Dark*. It was the first book I wrote on my phone. One week, I attended an insurance seminar at a Holiday Inn Express. It was for an insurance designation called the Certified Insurance Counselor (CIC), and the class was about general liability policies. The instructor was *amazing*, probably one of the best public speakers I've ever seen.

The class took breaks every hour for ten minutes so people could go to the bathroom and refresh their coffee and snacks.

On *every single break*, I power-walked to a nook near the hotel lobby, sat in a plushy chair, whipped out my phone, and wrote *Old Dark*. I probably wrote 5,000 or so words over three days just at the hotel on my phone—all during ten-minute breaks. I had a blast writing that novel. I passed the test at the end of the seminar too, which wasn't easy. After that seminar, I decided that if I was half as good as the teacher who taught that course, I'd be somebody.

(In a very ironic twist of fate, I became an instructor teaching the same material, and I even became an assistant vice president of general liability at a global insurance company. The passion started at the same time I was writing *Old Dark*. And even more ironic—I wrote *Old Dark* into the dark, which is a method of novel writing without outlining.)

When I look back on that moment, it was a signpost too. It cemented my ability to write on my phone. That conference forever broke my brain and changed my future. I learned how to execute on high levels with both writing and insurance. This is the point where both careers began to feed off each other.

In 2019, a brief minute I spent in an elevator was another. (I wrote about this in a previous chapter). That was the moment I learned to start owning the spiritual side of being a writer, and when I worked on my mindset and emotional baggage.

And now, in 2021, I've just passed another road sign. I reversed my focus from inward to outward after reading *The Conquest of Happiness*. Now I've landed an amazing job, published a metric ton of books, finished law school, and have a lot more time on my hands to shape my future. That's really exciting for me.

What are signposts saying? Hell if know. All I know is that I'm enjoying the ride, and at the very least, I'm not spinning my wheels.

What are your signposts?

THIS TIME LAST YEAR

I thought it would be fun to start a new segment that looks back at previous volumes to see how I have advanced and how the industry has changed. It's hard to believe that I'm already six volumes deep into this series and I am already forgetting what I wrote in earlier volumes.

What was happening a year ago in Q3 2020 ? Some of the things that were important for me:

- The world was still in partial lockdown due to the COVID-19 pandemic, but many in the US were starting to emerge for summer.
- The uncertainty about future events was palpable. It was impossible to plan for *anything*.
- Riots erupted all over the US after the murder of George Floyd.

Content Creation

. . .

This time last year, I was in the middle of my Beast Mode Challenge. Because I couldn't control current events, I focused on what I could control. I wrote over 100,000 words in August, even while a derecho (an inland hurricane) hit Iowa and knocked out power for several days.

I also did my second interview on "The Creative Penn," and my Internet connection crapped out on me during my chat with Joanna, which was a major embarrassment. Afterward, I immediately had Ethernet ports installed in my studio.

I also hired a video editor.

I also successfully narrated my first audiobook and got it approved on the first try.

Marketing

I implemented a new email signature with a headshot, title, and link to my books. That little decision (which cost about $40) is still paying off.

Technology and Data

I finished my automated sales database and was finding ways to visualize my data using Power BI.

Artificial intelligence was also top-of-mind. I wrote about natural language processing in that quarter's volume, which was the first step toward building my automated editing engine.

.   .   .

Writer of the Future

I wrote about the writing app of the future and how the writer of the future needs an app that functions as one command center, merging outlining, writing, editing, and formatting into one app so that the author (and editors and formatters) never have to leave the ecosystem. Today, one such writing app has emerged and is now in beta—Atticus (which I covered earlier in this book). While I wrote about this concept in 2020, I talked about it as early as 2019 on "The Writer's Journey" podcast. It's gratifying to see that someone else arrived at the same idea independently, especially one of brightest minds in publishing (Dave Chesson).

And, of course, I was still writing about bold new ideas that you can steal!

And here we are in 2021. What a year.

THIS TIME FIVE YEARS AGO

I was thinking about how far I've come compared to five years ago. I'll continue my trip into (not so) old memories.

In July 2016, my writing life was very different. I only had 17 books to my name, my YouTube channel was on a hiatus, and I was still struggling to figure out what direction I was going to take my writing business.

My most popular books had yet to be published: I had just finished *Old Dark* (*The Last Dragon Lord, Book 1*), but I had no idea how successful it was going to become.

I had just stopped outlining novels too. I wasn't making much money from my writing either. I hadn't started law school yet.

When I reflect on July 2016, I remember my processes and technology clearly:

I was using Scrivener two for Mac to write my novels.

- I was using Dragon for Mac to dictate. At this point, I had become proficient in dictation, using it to write *Old Dark*.

- Scrivener iOS had just released, allowing me to write on my phone. I was just starting to experiment with it.
- I was still using Scrivener's Compile feature to format ebooks.
- I gave up on paperback formatting because there wasn't a good formatting solution for Mac users. I had been playing around with professional templates, but none of them worked for me.
- I tracked my bookkeeping and sales manually. I don't even think I tracked my sales reports once in 2016 because it was such a pain.
- Artificial intelligence was just a buzzword. Everyone was experimenting with Facebook Ads, and they were the cheapest they would ever be.
- My book covers were all over the place. The designs were drastically different and I had inconsistent branding.

Yet I did a lot of things right in 2016, even though I wasn't aware at the time. Writing on my phone and dictation would lead to amazing word counts and the ability to continue my writing career. That year, I began a three-year campaign to create consistent branding on my book covers, finishing in 2019. Now all my covers have similar "shells." That was a huge leap forward.

Now Vellum is my formatting app and it has improved my paperback quality immensely.

I'm using automation in ways that I never would have dreamed of in 2016, although the technology was on computer and available back then.

Five years later in July 2021, I've come a long way and I have a lot to be proud of.

THIS TIME TEN YEARS AGO

Since we're on the topic of traveling back in time, I might as well look at the last decade...

The year was July 2011. I had been out of college for a year and was working a crappy job as a claims adjuster. The silver lining was that I had become bilingual in Spanish on the job. My Spanish was very good.

I was writing poetry at the time, and I had just started meeting with a writer friend at a coffee shop on Tuesdays. We shared our work and talked shop.

I despised self-publishing. Sometime around this period, I went to an open mic night and heard a poet who delivered a fantastic poem on stage. He ended by saying that he had a book on Amazon. I loved the poem, so I bought his collection. A week later, a monstrosity of a book appeared in my mailbox. The cover looked as if it had been designed in Microsoft Paint, the text was full of typos, and the formatting was unprofessional. I swore that I would never buy another self-published book, and I believed that an author *needed* a publisher behind them.

I know that's hard to believe that I was ever anti-self-publishing, but I wrote an entry in my journal about it, and I'm embarrassed to share it with you, but here it is:

━━

I have known a few people to self-publish their work. I recently had a friend who published a novel. Finishing a novel is to be commended. Everyone wants to write the next great novel, but most of us aren't writers, most of us can't do it, and most of us shouldn't even try. However, I respect those who do it and give it their all, no matter what the quality of their work. But self-publishing is the worst way to celebrate the finishing of your work...

Authors who self-publish are driven by the belief that their novel is going to be epic, and that it's going to change the world. Unless you've got an editor and an audience, it won't. For the aspiring author, it's one of the most foolish things you can do. First, self-published books brand you as an amateur. Second, self-publishing a novel ensures that it especially won't be picked up by a publishing house—publishers want to be the first to publish a work. Don't make it hard on yourself. Self-publishing is essentially the same as tossing your book into a river.

━━

Keep in mind that this was a private journal entry, and I was so smug and condescending...and also keep in mind that I had barely written a few poems around this time. It's embarrassing, but we all have said and done things in our past that we believed at the time but disavow now. I find the passage above embarrassing but also an indicator of how I've evolved over the years.

I had no idea that I would have a near-death experience one

year later in July 2012, and it would change my perspective on writing forever. I was a year away from a paradigm shift.

It's amazing how far you can go in a decade. That's why I like to think in terms of years and decades. It's easy to overestimate what you can do in a year while also underestimating what you can do in a decade. What types of goals would my 2011 self have made for 2021?

I might have wanted to write 100 poems thinking that it would take me 10 years. That's 10 poems per year. I was a perfectionist back then. With a perfectionist mindset, it's not hard to see how you could limit yourself to such a small number...and still not get published in magazines. I suffered from self-doubt too. I rewrote *everything* and took advice from anyone and everyone who read my work, even people who didn't even like poetry.

Again, it's amazing what a difference a decade makes.

As I think about my progress through 2031 (ten years from now), what are my goals?

I have no idea what will happen throughout the next decade. But if I'm able, I plan to keep writing. If I write 10 books per year, I'll have published *at least* 160 books by then. Who knows, maybe I'll increase my writing output dramatically and be well over 200 by that time. Or maybe I'll suffer a setback and be at a significantly lower number. Or, maybe everything I wrote in this paragraph will be hilariously wrong.

If I'm lucky, I'll be a full-time writer by 2031, with no debt, house paid off, and a fair amount saved up for retirement. My parents will be aging, so I will have the responsibility of taking care of them, something I started preparing for in 2014. My daughter will be in high school and I'll be looking at an empty nest very soon—and booooy, if you thought I was a fast writer now, wait until I don't have to worry about kids in the house anymore...

I hope this series will continue for ten years so I can verify if anything I wrote was correct.

Q3 PROGRESS REPORT

In the previous volume, I shared the progress I was making toward my 2021 author strategy. This strategy will guide me for the next several years. I wanted to provide an update for Q2 2021.

MY STRATEGY

My mission is to educate and entertain my audience in the genres I write, and to remain nimble in an ever-changing industry.

I will achieve my mission through five strategic priorities:

- Become a world-class content creator
- Become a world-class marketer
- Become a technology-driven writer
- Become a data-driven writer
- Become the writer of the future

WORLD-CLASS CONTENT CREATOR

Goal: 64 books published by 12/31/2021. I'm currently at 58 books written (including this one), which is approximately 89 percent to plan. I'm writing this in July and have approximately half the year left. Beast Mode will help me exceed my plan this year.

Develop a way to ensure consistency across my platform. Not started.

WORLD-CLASS MARKETER

Grow my Amazon Ad imprint. Completed.

Improve my copywriting skills. Completed.

Reduce my tax liability. Successfully failed (and completed). See the previous volume for more information.

BECOME A TECHNOLOGY-DRIVEN WRITER

Develop an automated way to enforce consistency. Completed.

Redesign my Book Wizard tool on Michael La Ronn.com and Author Level Up.com. Not started. Hopefully, I'll achieve it in Q4.

Implement a flexible book database that houses all the metadata for my books. Not started. I may not accomplish the goal this year, so if that happens, I'll push it to 2022.

Automate my bookkeeping. Successfully completed.

BECOME A DATA-DRIVEN WRITER

Make minor enhancements to my sales database. Not started.

Invest in learning the basics of Python, Webhooks, and Application Programming Interfaces (APIs). I took an API course in Q1, which was very helpful and informative. I will complete this goal in Q4. I should accomplish it easily.

BECOME THE WRITER OF THE FUTURE

Read 50 books. I'm still at 50 percent toward the goal, with around 20 books read this year. I may fall just short of plan.

Implement direct print and audiobook sales onto my website. Not started.

Complete my law degree. Completed.

Complete 12 WMG workshops to improve my writing craft. I'm in danger of missing this goal as I still haven't started yet.

BRINGING IT ALL TOGETHER

.   .   .

I wrote this volume early in the quarter, so my progress is a little thin. I expect to have more completed in Q4.

I don't have all my goals listed here, but for the ones I do, I have achieved 6 out of 15, which is 40 percent.

I'm on track to completing two others, so that brings my completion to 53 percent.

For me, I'll have a rock-solid year if I hit around a 75 percent completion rate. I always set more goals than I can accomplish to help me stay motivated. The goals I accomplished are pretty big ones too.

I don't care if I miss goals. I prefer to set many goals; if I accomplish half of them, I've had an amazing year. I'm not stressing over them.

I'll share more progress on my strategy in the next volume so I can keep myself accountable, but you can view the details of my 2021+ strategy by visiting www.authorlevelup.com/2021strategy

CONTENT CREATED WHILE WRITING THIS BOOK

Books

Authors, Steal This Book: 67 Business Ideas for the Writers of the Future

In this book, M.L. Ronn breaks down 67 radical ideas that might just change the future of the writing profession as we know it. This book is free because ideas are meant to be shared. You might find something on these pages that could change your writing career.

Buy at www.authorlevelup.com/stealthisbook.

READ THE NEXT VOLUME

Michael's writer journey continues in the next volume of this series!

Grab your copy at www.authorlevelup.com/confidential.

MEET M.L. RONN

Science fiction and fantasy on the wild side!

M.L. Ronn (Michael La Ronn) is the author of many science fiction and fantasy novels including *The Good Necromancer*, *Android X*, and *The Last Dragon Lord* series.

In 2012, a life-threatening illness made him realize that storytelling was his #1 passion. He's devoted his life to writing ever since, making up whatever story makes him fall out of his chair laughing the hardest. Every day.

Learn more about Michael
www.authorlevelup.com (for writers)
www.michaellaronn.com (fiction)

MORE BOOKS BY M.L. RONN

Books for Writers:

www.authorlevelup.com/books

Fiction:

www.michaellaronn.com/books